# Aeronautical Knowledge – Operational Procedures

**2nd Edition**

**Jeremy M Pratt**

ISBN 978-1-80035-042-7

Published by:
Airplan Flight Equipment Ltd

This book is a guide to the CAA and EASA Operational Procedures Theoretical Knowledge syllabus for the Private Pilot Licence (PPL) and Light Aircraft Pilot Licence (LAPL) for aeroplanes.

This book is not intended to be an authoritative document and it does not in any way over-rule or counter instruction from an approved or registered training organisation or information or guidance produced by the Civil Aviation Authority (CAA), European Aviation Safety Agency (EASA) or by any other Competent Authority. Full reference should be made to applicable UK and EU regulations, Implementing Regulations and Acceptable Means of Compliance and Guidance Material (AMC/GM). Rules, procedures, limitations and guidance in documents produced by Competent Authorities, including but not limited to national law and guidance, Aeronautical Information Publications (AIP), Aeronautical Information Circulars (AIC) and the applicable Aircraft Flight Manual (AFM) – alternatively the Pilots Operating Handbook/Flight Manual (POH/FM) – must also be complied with at all times. Requirements of the aircraft operator, for example in an Operations Manual or flying order book, must also be complied with.

At the end of 2020 the UK formally left EASA; however for practical purposes EU and EASA regulations have been taken into UK law and there are few practical differences between UK and EASA aviation law. Where there are significant differences, these are noted in the 'National Procedures' section of this book.

Aeronautical information, including that relating to Operational Procedures, can – and does – change frequently and it is the pilot's responsibility to remain up-to-date with such changes. The provisions of good airmanship and safe operating practice should be adhered to at all times.

Whilst every care has been taken in compiling this publication, relying where possible on authoritative and official information sources, the publisher and editorial team will not be liable in any way for any errors or omission whatsoever.

First edition 2017

Second edition 2021



Aeronautical Knowledge – Operational Procedures

2nd Edition

ISBN 978-1-80035-042-7

Printed in Malta by Melita Press

**Airplan Flight Equipment Ltd**
1a Ringway Trading Estate,
Shadowmoss Road,
Manchester M22 5LH UK

**www.afeonline.com**

# Contents

# Foreword and acknowledgements

This publication provides the Theoretical Knowledge (TK) required in Operational Procedures for non-commercial flight operations under Visual Flight Rules (VFR). It is based on the 2015 PPL and LAPL Theoretical Knowledge (TK) Operational Procedures syllabus published by the UK CAA and accepted by EASA and it is considered suitable for use in conjunction with training courses for the following pilot licences:

- EASA Private Pilot Licence (PPL) (Aeroplane)
- EASA Light Aircraft Pilot Licence (LAPL) (Aeroplane)
- CAA Private Pilot Licence (PPL) (Aeroplane)
- CAA Light Aircraft Pilot Licence (LAPL) (Aeroplane)
- UK National PPL (NPPL) (Aeroplane)
- ICAO-compliant PPL (Aeroplane) or equivalent licence
- Core knowledge for EASA and CAA Commercial Pilot Licence (CPL) (Aeroplane)
- Foundation knowledge for EASA and CAA Airline Transport Pilot Licence (ATPL) (Aeroplane)
- Foundation knowledge for EASA and CAA Multi-crew Pilot Licence (MPL) (Aeroplane)

This publication also provides foundation knowledge for an Air Transport Operations/ Management degree or similar academic qualification.

# About the Author

Jeremy M Pratt took his first flying lesson at the age of 14, paid for by working in the hangar and radio unit at his local airfield. He gained his pilot's licence shortly after his 18th birthday after being awarded an Esso/Air League Flying Scholarship, became a flying instructor at 19 and a commercial pilot at the age of 20.

Since then he has taught (and continues to teach) pilots for a wide range of licences – both private and professional – as well as associated ratings and qualifications including night, instrument, tailwheel and multi-engine flying and he has flown General Aviation aircraft professionally in a number of other roles including pleasure flights, traffic reporting, aerial photography and aerial survey. He has owned and co-owned a number of General Aviation aircraft and flown a variety of aircraft types from Tiger Moth biplane to Cessna Citation jet, as well as trying-out helicopter, microlight and balloon flying. He also enjoys the highs (and occasional lows) of flying gliders.

The author's first flying training books were published in 1992, since when they have sold several hundred thousand copies world-wide and have been translated into a number of languages. He has also authored and co-authored around 25 additional aviation training books as well as contributing to various aviation publications including Flight Training News (FTN), for which he flight tests various aircraft types.

The author works with various aviation authorities and organisations on training and safety issues. He was also part of the team that produced the 2015 CAA/EASA PPL and LAPL syllabi and he sits on the CAA's PPL Theoretical Knowledge Working Group. He flies whenever he can find the time – for instructing, for business, for pleasure and for the sheer joy of flight.

# Image Acknowledgements



## OP1 Application of Threat and Error Management

OP1.1 courtesy BBC; OP1.2 © BanksPhotos; OP1.3 © AFE; OP1.4 © AFE; OP1.5 © Gos Eye View; OP1.6 © Franc Vrtacnik; OP1.7 © Cirrus Design; OP1.8 © AFE; OP1.9 © Camrocker/AFE; OP1.10 © Gabriel Savit; OP1.11 © AFE; OP1.12 © AFE

## OP2 Operation of Aircraft

OP2.1 © Pilatus Aircraft Ltd; OP2.2 © Tecnam; OP2.3 Courtesy CAA; OP2.4 Vasilyev Alexandr; OP2.5 Courtesy Met. Office; OP2.6 © AFE; OP2.7 © Tecnam; OP2.8 Courtesy CAA; OP2.9 © AFE; OP2.10 Courtesy Falcon Flight Academy; OP2.11 © CAA; OP2.12 © NITO; OP2.13 © AS-kom; OP2.14 Courtesy Gemplers.com; OP2.15 © AFE; OP2.16 © oneinchpunch; OP2.17 © WRU Party; OP2.18 © Crown Copyright; OP2.19 © Cirrus Design; OP2.20 © Avco Corporation; OP2.21 © AFE; OP2.22 © AFE; OP2.23 © AFE; OP2.24 © AFE; OP2.25 © AFE; OP2.26 © AFE; OP2.27 © AFE; OP2.28 © AFE; OP2.29 © AFE; OP2.30 © AFE; OP2.31 © AFE; OP2.32 © AFE; OP2.33 © AFE; OP2.34 © AFE; OP2.35 © AFE; OP2.36 © AFE; OP2.37 © AFE; OP2.38 Courtesy H3R Aviation; OP2.39 courtesy ASA; OP2.40 © AFE; OP2.41 © McMurdo; OP2.42 © AFE; OP2.43 © McMurdo; OP2.44 © Seago; OP2.45 © Seago; OP2.46 © AFE; OP2.47 Courtesy flusi.info

## OP3 Avoidance of Hazards

OP3.1 © AFE; OP3.2 © Derek Pedley; OP3.3 © Richard Whitcombe; OP3.4 © AFE; OP3.5 Courtesy AOPA.org; OP3.6 Courtesy SkyDemon; OP3.7 © dragunov; OP3.8 © AFE; OP3.9 © NASA; OP3.9a © Jorgen Syversen; OP3.9b; OP3.10 © AFE; OP3.11 © 'Hargreaves'; OP3.12 © AFE; OP3.13 © 'Hargreaves'; OP3.14 © AFE; OP3.15 © 'Hargreaves'; OP3.16 © 'Hargreaves'; OP3.17 © Jorgen Syversen; OP3.18 © AFE; OP3.19 © Javi Sanchez Utzet; OP3.20 © Markus Mainka; OP3.21 © Rebius; OP3.22 © Fasttailwind; OP3.23 © Olaf Schulz; OP3.24 Courtesy Textron; OP3.25 © AFE; OP3.26 © AFE; OP3.27 © AFE; OP3.28 © AFE

## OP4 Search and Rescue Procedures

OP4.1 © AFE Ltd; OP4.2 © AFE Ltd; OP4.3 UKN; OP4.5 UKN; OP4.5© AFE; OP4.6 © AFE; OP4.7 © AFE; OP4.8 © Simon Willson; OP4.9 © AFE

## OP5 Accidents and Incidents

OP5.1 © AFE; OP5.2 © AFE; OP5.3 Courtesy EASA; OP5.4 Courtesy CHIRP; OP5.5 Courtesy belgocontro; OP5.6 Courtesy EGAST; OP5.7 Courtesy Clued Up

## OP6 Care of Passengers

OP6.1a © AFE; OP6.1b © AFE; OP6.2 © AFE; OP6.3a © AFE; OP6.3b © AFE; OP6.4a © AFE; OP6.4b © AFE, OP6.4c © AFE; OP6.5a © AFE; OP6.5b © AFE; OP6.6a © AFE; OP6.6b © AFE; OP6.7a © AFE; OP6.7b © AFE

## OP7 National Procedures

OP7.1 © Crown Copyright; OP7.2 © CAA; OP7.3 Hollowaynaughton; OP7.4 © TRIG Avionics; OP7.5 © AFE; OP7.6 © AFE; OP7.7 © AFE; OP7.8 © AFE; OP7.9 © AFE; OP7.10 © Crown Copyright; OP7.11 Courtesy EASA; OP7.12 Courtesy CAA; OP7.13 Courtesy UKAB; OP7.14 Courtesy CHIRP; OP7.15 Courtesy CAA; OP7.16 Courtesy GASCo

# Acknowledgements

Creating a book is, rather like flying itself, an activity that needs the help and assistance of a whole range of people to bring the dream into reality. I have been fortunate over the years to have met, flown and worked with a range of very talented people in both the aviation and publishing worlds and many of them have, in one way or another, contributed to this book. The following are just some of the people and organisations who have directly contributed or worked on this book, and I offer my heartfelt thanks to them. To any person or organisation I may have inadvertently missed out, I additionally offer my apologies for the oversight.

Air Accidents Investigation Branch (AAIB)

Airplan Flight Equipment (AFE)

Air Team Images

Wendy Barratt

Brighton City Airport

Civil Aviation Authority

CHIRP

GASCo

Rob Taylor – GDi Studio

Sky Demon

Dave Unwin

And, of course, my long-suffering family who continue to tolerate my obsession for all things flying for reasons I've never fully understood.

The appropriate image and photograph permissions and copyrights are listed in the 'Image Acknowledgements' section.

*It is possible to fly without motors, but not without knowledge and skill.*
Wilbur Wright

# Introduction

When the theoretical knowledge subject of 'Operational Procedures' first appeared in the PPL and LAPL syllabus, it was greeted with a fair degree of head-scratching amongst the flying instructor community. To some, this part of the syllabus seemed to have been cobbled together with bits of knowledge borrowed from other theoretical knowledge subjects, with no obvious common thread.

With the advent of the 2015 PPL & LAPL syllabus, a lot of these concerns were allayed by focussing on subjects which had direct application to the day-to-day operation of General Aviation (GA) aircraft – including practical skills and knowledge such as aircraft refuelling, the use of safety equipment, dangerous goods and the responsibilities of the Pilot-in-Command (PIC). Other important subjects which have previously been rather neglected in non-commercial pilot training are also now covered, such as the care of passengers, a subject which up until now was left to the pilot to pick-up once they had a licence and were flying with passengers for the first time – hardly ideal!

The updated syllabus also introduces knowledge of the 'Part-NCO' regulations, a set of rules governing the non-commercial operation of non-complex aircraft. A lot of the Part-NCO rules set out formally the sort of 'best practice' and safety procedures which a pilot otherwise might have to pick-up from good flight instruction and the example of more experienced pilots. Clearly the earlier a pilot is introduced to these practices, the more competent and capable that pilot will be.

The current 'Operational Procedures' syllabus also takes the opportunity to introduce the concept of 'Threat and Error Management' (TEM). TEM was first developed in the airline industry in the 1990s, and later adopted into professional pilot training. TEM has now found its way into PPL and LAPL training and in this book I have adapted established TEM techniques for a non-commercial, General Aviation flying. In many ways, TEM is just a modern embodiment of the sort of 'defensive thinking' which has gone under a number of different terms in the past, such as risk management and safety culture. It is generally accepted nowadays that there is no such thing as a risk-free operation, instead the focus has to be on anticipating and predicting potential problems and coming-up with a strategy for dealing with them.

On a similar note, the section on 'Avoidance of Hazards' focusses on the most common hazards a General Aviation pilot may face in day-to-day flying situations, and how best to prepare for them. In the aviation business the idiom 'prevention is better than cure' is particularly apt. It is one of the signs of competent pilots that they recognise and anticipate hazards and unnecessary risks, and avoid them wherever possible. This approach to flying is far superior to getting into endless 'scrapes' and 'close calls', then relying on luck and every reserve of piloting skill to escape a situation the pilot could have easily avoided in the first place.

I hope that by concentrating on the practical aspects of aircraft operation, this subject will be seen as an aid to practical flying, rather than an academic subject with little real-world application. The safe operation of aircraft requires both skill and knowledge from the pilot in equal measure, and the best pilots view the improvement and development of both these attributes as a career-long journey, rather than a one-off effort to pass a test.

Jeremy M Pratt
May 2021

# OP1 Application of Threat and Error Management

**Threat and Error Management (TEM) in aircraft operation**

**Progress check**

# Application of Threat and Error Management

## Threat and Error Management (TEM) in aircraft operation

The concept of **Threat and Error Management** (**TEM**) grew out of a safety study between a large university and a major airline in the 1990s. As a result of this study TEM techniques were developed and taught to flight crews on a one-day course. A follow-up study showed a significant reduction in flight crew errors and the rate of certain unsafe situations fell by 70%. Based on this success, the concept of TEM was adopted as 'best practice' by the International Civil Aviation Organisation (ICAO). Although TEM has its origins in airline safety, its basic principles can be applied to all types of flying activity and TEM training is now an ICAO standard for all levels of pilot licences (as well as for Air Traffic Controllers). What follows is a basic guide to TEM for a General Aviation (GA) pilot operating an aircraft which only needs a one-person flight crew.

In TEM, a '**threat**' is an external factor outside the control of the pilot which makes the operation of the aircraft more complex or introduces an element of risk. A 'threat' needs to be recognised and managed in order to maintain an acceptable level of safety.

A prime example of a 'threat' is weather. The weather is clearly an external force outside the control of the pilot (or any other person!), but weather can have a direct influence on the safety of a flight. Some threats caused by weather are so severe that avoidance is the only sensible course of action for a GA pilot – for example an active thunderstorm or dense fog. Other weather threats may be more subtle – at times a pilot may need to consider the effect of low cloud or reduced visibility. Can the planned flight be completed safely and legally? What alternative courses of action are available to maintain a good margin of safety?

Figure OP1.1
Bad weather is one of the potential external 'threats' a pilot has to consider.

Figure OP1.2
The risk of coming into conflict with other aircraft is another example of a 'threat' (although these aircraft are actually practicing formation flying)

Another common 'threat' is that of conflict with other aircraft. GA aircraft often operate in uncontrolled airspace and even when inside controlled airspace, a VFR flight is usually responsible for maintaining its own separation from other aircraft. The pilot will need to consider factors which increase the threat of conflict with other aircraft (eg busy airfields, popular VFR routes avoiding controlled airspace) and adopt measures to minimise that risk – for example maintaining a good lookout and obtaining an ATC radar service.

A 'threat' may also come from less obvious sources. Flying over hostile terrain – such as high ground or the sea – introduces some element of extra complexity and risk to a flight. The aircraft design itself may have certain features which could be a 'threat' in specific situations. An aircraft designed to have a fast cruise speed may not have good 'short field' take-off and landing performance, so operation from a short runway needs careful consideration. In most aircraft it is not possible to fill all the seats, all the luggage capacity and also fill the fuel tanks. The pilot will need to consider the effect that a reduced fuel load will have on range and endurance. Can the planned route be completed in one flight, or will a fuel stop be necessary to maintain adequate fuel reserves? Equipment malfunction is also a 'threat'. Some malfunctions may be minor and pose little or no risk to a flight, whereas an unexpected major malfunction may require immediate action by the pilot.

Figure OP1.3
Sometimes poor design can represent a 'threat' – such as this ambiguous fuel selector on a vintage aircraft.

Figure OP1.4
An inoperative item of equipment can also represent a 'Threat' – in this case equipment malfunction.

Because a 'threat' is outside the control of the pilot, it is highly unlikely that any flight can be completely free of threat, in fact studies have shown that an average airline operation encounters around four threats per flight. In the less regulated world of GA flying, that figure is probably higher due to factors such as uncontrolled and uncertified airfields, operations in uncontrolled airspace and different standards of aircraft design, equipment and maintenance which are rarely applicable to airline operations. An important element of the TEM concept is to accept that threats cannot be entirely eliminated or avoided and so require careful attention from the pilot. A vigilant pilot will be assessing potential threats beginning at the pre-flight planning stage, throughout the flight and all the way through to completing paperwork at the end of the flight. At any point a pilot should be asking him or her-self: what are the threats, what can I do about them and what are my alternative courses of action?

While threats are factors external to the pilot, 'errors' are very much a pilot factor. Within TEM, an '**error**' is a pilot action (or lack of action) which leads to a situation the pilot did not intend or expect. An 'error' reduces safety and increases the risk of an incident or accident.

In the past, there was an emphasis in aviation (and other comparable industries) of seeking to eliminate human error completely, especially through the use of technology. TEM takes the more enlightened view that in any human activity, some level of 'error' is inevitable. An 'error' that is minor and is quickly recognised and corrected by the pilot is a feature of almost any flight a pilot will ever make. An 'error' that is not recognised, or is deliberately ignored by the pilot, is a less normal and more risky matter.

Figure OP1.5
An 'error' can be the result of an action, or inaction, by the pilot.

Figure OP1.6
Errors in the handling of the aircraft controls are a common form of error.

An 'error' can take many different forms. Probably the most serious errors are those that involve the actual flying of the aircraft. Such handling errors may occur because a pilot lacks the training or skill to complete a particular manoeuvre safely and the risk of such an 'error' occurring is increased if a pilot is not in current practice. Common sense tells us that if a pilot has not practiced a glide approach for many years, that pilot is less likely make a safe glide approach and landing than a pilot who has regularly practiced glide approaches. A handling error may be more subtle – for example using an incorrect technique for a short-field take-off, or not properly operating the fuel system. In any event, a handling error that is not recognised and corrected will reduce the safety margin of a flight.

Another form of 'error' is a procedural error. In General Aviation operations such an 'error' might consist of misreading a checklist, not following an established circuit pattern or loading an aircraft outside its limits. In General Aviation operations, procedures may be established by the aircraft operator (for example, a flying school) but where an aircraft is privately owned and operated, such established procedures are less likely to exist. The over-riding procedures will normally be those set out by the aircraft manufacturer in a document known as the Aircraft Flight Manual (AFM) – alternatively in the Pilots Operating Handbook/ Flight Manual (POH/FM). This document will detail the aircraft's characteristics, systems, limitations and operating procedures and the aircraft's checklist will be based on this document. Operating the aircraft in contravention of the AFM is a significant procedural 'error'. Aviation regulations (such as the Rules of the Air) establish overall operating procedures and additional procedures may also apply at individual airfields – for example circuit patterns, local flying areas, taxiing routes etc. It is the pilot's responsibility to be aware of regulations and operating procedures and comply with them. There are also less formalised procedures which can be considered to be 'best practice'. For example, before entering a runway it is good practice to look both ways to ensure that the runway and approaches are clear, regardless of any ATC clearance.

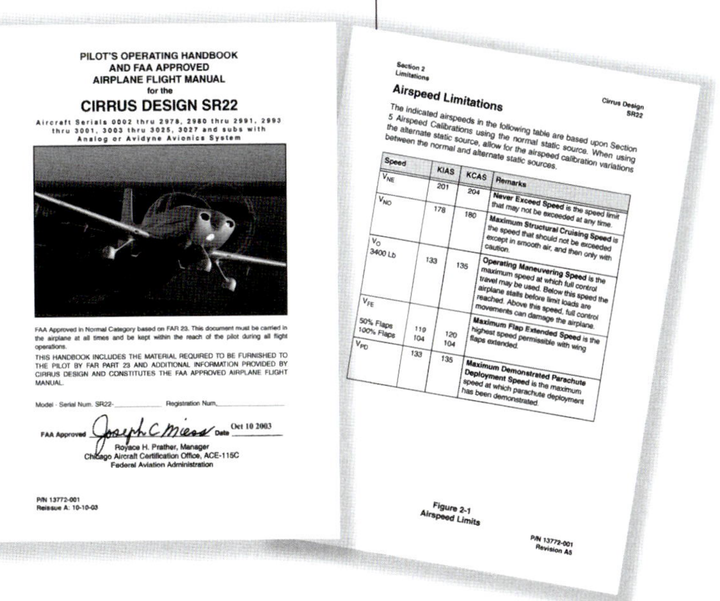

PILOT'S OPERATING HANDBOOK
AND FAA APPROVED
AIRPLANE FLIGHT MANUAL
for the
CIRRUS DESIGN SR22

Aircraft Serials 0002 thru 2978, 2980 thru 2991, 2993 thru 3001, 3003 thru 3025, 3027 and subs with Analog or Avidyne Avionics System

FAA Approved in Normal Category based on FAR 23. This document must be carried in the airplane at all times and be kept within the reach of the pilot during all flight operations.

THIS HANDBOOK INCLUDES THE MATERIAL REQUIRED TO BE FURNISHED TO THE PILOT BY FAR PART 23 AND ADDITIONAL INFORMATION PROVIDED BY CIRRUS DESIGN AND CONSTITUTES THE FAA APPROVED AIRPLANE FLIGHT MANUAL.

Model - Serial Num. SR22-________ Registration Num.________

FAA Approved [signature] Date Oct 10 2003
Royace H. Prather, Manager
Chicago Aircraft Certification Office, ACE-115C
Federal Aviation Administration

P/N 13772-001
Reissue A: 10-10-03

Section 2
Limitations

Cirrus Design
SR22

**Airspeed Limitations**

The indicated airspeeds in the following table are based upon Section 5 Airspeed Calibrations using the normal static source. When using the alternate static source, allow for the airspeed calibration variations between the normal and alternate static sources.

| Speed | KIAS | KCAS | Remarks |
|---|---|---|---|
| $V_{NE}$ | 201 | 204 | **Never Exceed Speed** is the speed limit that may not be exceeded at any time. |
| $V_{NO}$ | 178 | 180 | **Maximum Structural Cruising Speed** is the speed that should not be exceeded except in smooth air, and then only with caution. |
| $V_O$ 3400 Lb | 133 | 135 | **Operating Maneuvering Speed** is the maximum speed at which full control travel may be used. Below this speed the airplane stalls before limit loads are reached. Above this speed, full control movements can damage the airplane. |
| $V_{FE}$ 50% Flaps 100% Flaps | 119 104 | 120 104 | **Maximum Flap Extended Speed** is the highest speed permissible with wing flaps extended. |
| $V_{PD}$ | 133 | 135 | **Maximum Demonstrated Parachute Deployment Speed** is the maximum speed at which parachute deployment has been demonstrated. |

Figure 2-1
Airspeed Limits

P/N 13772-001
Revision A5

Figure OP1.7
Operating the aircraft in accordance with its approved procedures and limitations is an important means to reduce 'errors'.

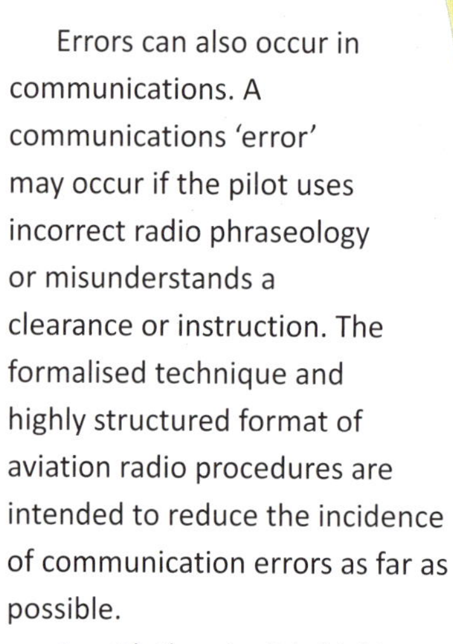


Figure OP1.8
Using the aircraft checklist will significantly reduce the risk of 'errors'.

Errors can also occur in communications. A communications 'error' may occur if the pilot uses incorrect radio phraseology or misunderstands a clearance or instruction. The formalised technique and highly structured format of aviation radio procedures are intended to reduce the incidence of communication errors as far as possible.

As with threats, it is highly unlikely that any flight can ever be completely error-free. Studies suggest that airline operations include around three errors per flight and there is no reason to think that an average GA flight would have fewer errors. The focus of the pilot should be to be alert for errors, and correct any errors as soon as they are recognised.

To summarise, 'threats' come at the pilot, 'errors' come from the pilot.

Figure OP1.9
Threats come at the pilot, errors come from the pilot.

Figure OP1.10
An 'Undesired Aircraft State'. The pilot did not intend the aircraft to end-up on the ground with its undercarriage up.

If a threat and/or an error is not properly managed, the result may be an '**undesired aircraft state**'. An undesired aircraft state means that the aircraft is either in the wrong place, at the wrong speed, at the wrong attitude or in the wrong configuration, or in some combination of these undesired states. The most extreme instance of an undesired aircraft state would be the pilot losing control of the aircraft; but other examples could include being too high and too fast on approach, being low on fuel or infringing controlled airspace.

Again relying on studies of airline operations, at least 30% of undesired aircraft states occur as a result of a chain of events that started with a threat that was not properly managed, which led to an error or series of errors. This is a feature of safety incidents and accidents, they very rarely happen though a single cause or event, but are almost always the result of a number of factors and very often, the chain of threat(s) and error(s) leading to an incident or accident could have been interrupted at any number of points. Clearly, the earlier the chain or threats and/or errors is broken, the better.

Based very loosely on the theories of Herbert Heinrich (author of the 1931 book *Industrial Accident Prevention, A Scientific Approach*), a safety triangle can be constructed. At the lowest level are 3,000 threats or errors. If these are not managed properly they may lead to the next level, 300 instances of undesired aircraft states. Failure to correct these 300 undesired aircraft states could lead to 29 incidents and in turn, one of those incidents has the potential to become an aircraft accident. The principle of TEM is to intervene at the earliest possible stage in the process, so that threats and errors cannot cause an undesired aircraft state and lead to a more serious outcome.

Figure OP1.11
Failure to deal with minor threats and errors can lead to bigger problems.

For a pilot to apply good TEM techniques, the key actions required are ***anticipation***, ***recognition*** and ***recovery***.

***Anticipation*** is a matter of expecting that threats and errors will occur. This expectation should start at the pre-flight planning stage and continue right through to the process of completing paperwork at the end of the flight. From this expectation the pilot becomes alert to threats and errors both potential and actual.

***Recognition*** is the vital action of identifying that a threat or error has occurred. Recognition becomes easier with increased knowledge and experience. It is sometimes said that experience gives the pilot the capacity to recognise a mistake when it is made again. However, recognising a threat or an error is no use without the third action.

***Recovery*** is the logical next step after recognition. Having recognised a threat or error, the pilot takes action to prevent, or recover from, an undesired aircraft state. Recovery must always be the imperative, overriding, course of action following recognition. Once recovery has taken place, the pilot can then analyse what went wrong (using TEM techniques) and take further actions or preventative measures as necessary.

Always recover first, ask questions later.

Good TEM skills are developed gradually and with practice and experience. Starting to think in TEM terms at the pre-flight planning stage of a flight is an efficient way of avoiding or mitigating factors before they become significant. Sometimes the most important decisions a pilot makes occur long before ever getting airborne. Before flight, a simple TEM review might be:

- What are the threats?
- What are the errors?
- How will I manage them?

At the end of a flight, TEM can be reinforced by taking a couple of minutes to review the flight, again in TEM terms:

- What were the threats?
- What were the errors?
- How did I manage them?
- What would I do differently next time?

This approach to actions before and after flight is consistent with the common practice of carrying out some form of '**briefing**' before a flight. Even for a single pilot flying alone, such a pre-flight brief is important to establish in the pilot's own mind what the flight is intended to achieve and how the flight will be conducted. Just as importantly, a '**debrief**' after the flight – a post-flight review of what went right and what went wrong – is invaluable in learning lessons from the flight and building experience.

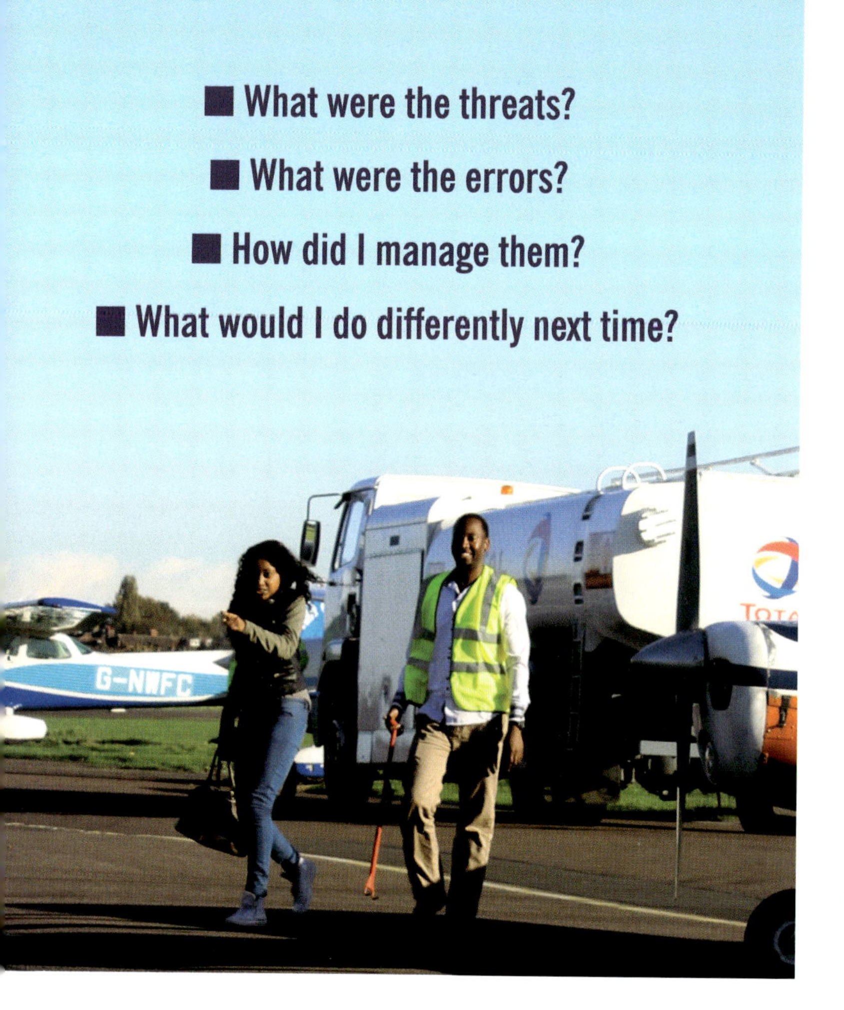


Figure OP1.12
The post-flight debrief may be as simple as considering a few basic questions.
*"Nothing is a waste of time if you use the experience wisely."* (Auguste Rodin).

The process of TEM is sometimes confused with certain desirable pilot attributes, one of which is 'situational awareness'. In flying terms **situational awareness** is a matter of having an accurate understanding of the current situation, the environment around the aircraft and what is likely to occur in the immediate future. By applying good TEM techniques a pilot is likely to exercise the vigilance and anticipation necessary to develop good situational awareness, which is not something that happens quickly for most pilots. Good situational awareness requires sufficient spare mental capacity to think beyond the immediate task of flying the aircraft, consider other factors around the aircraft and anticipate how events are likely to develop. Few pilots have this sort of spare capacity at the beginning of a flying course, but with practice and growing experience, exercising sound TEM techniques will help to nurture situational awareness.

TEM is also sometimes talked about as a replacement for 'airmanship'. According to ICAO, **airmanship** is "*...the consistent use of good judgment and well-developed skills to accomplish flight objectives.*" A pilot who is using good TEM techniques can be said to be also exercising good airmanship, but that is not the same as replacing airmanship with TEM. Recognising a threat (for example the danger of airborne conflict with other aircraft) and managing that threat with appropriate action (for example maintaining a good lookout), is just one area where good TEM leads to good airmanship. In general it is true to say that exercising good TEM leads to good airmanship – in other words TEM is a method of achieving good airmanship. For many pilots, though, airmanship goes a step further and involves not only well-developed skills and judgement, but also consideration for others. A pilot who checks behind the aircraft before carrying out power checks, or takes care to avoid noise-sensitive areas when carrying out stalls and steep turns, is certainly exercising good airmanship (as a result of good situational awareness) and that has to be a good thing.

In conclusion, Threat and Error Management (TEM) is a process, a way of thinking, which will help the pilot anticipate and recognise threats and errors, avoid an undesired aircraft state where possible and recover from it when necessary. Many drivers are familiar with the concept of 'defensive driving', the process of driving in such a way to reduce danger by anticipating dangerous scenarios. If you think of TEM as a form of defensive flying you will recognise that TEM is about minimising risks and maximising safety margins. Pilots are often the 'last line of defence' in aviation safety, and never more so than in single pilot, general aviation operations. A pilot who uses good TEM techniques is best placed to minimise risk, maximise safety margins and stay out of trouble.

## Progress check

1. In terms of aviation Threat and Error Management, what is a 'threat'?
2. Give an example of a common aviation 'threat'
3. In terms of aviation Threat and Error Management, what is an 'error'?
4. Give an example of a common aviation 'error'.
5. What is an 'undesired aircraft state'?
6. What are the key actions required for a pilot to apply good Threat and Error Management (TEM) techniques?
7. What is 'situational awareness'?
8. What is 'airmanship'?

These questions are intended to test knowledge and reinforce some of the key learning points from this section. In answering these questions, a 'pass rate' of around 80% should be the target.

Model answers are found at page 98.

# OP2 Operation of Aircraft

Applicability of aviation regulations

Responsibility and authority of the Pilot-in-Command (PIC)

Documents to be carried

Dangerous goods

Fuel and oil, refuelling

Instruments and equipment

Safety equipment

Progress check

# OP2 Operation of Aircraft

## Applicability of aviation regulations

Regulations regarding the operation of aircraft are found in various aviation regulations, which are so-called 'hard law'; their provisions are mandatory and not negotiable. Each of the relevant regulations are supported by Acceptable Means of Compliance/Guidance Material (AMC/GM). For the non-commercial operation of aircraft, the AMC/GMs can be viewed as guidance and advice on how to comply with the relevant regulation

The following information focuses on the Visual Flight Rules (VFR) operation of non commercial flights in 'other than complex' aircraft.

A complex motor-powered aeroplane means an aeroplane:

- with a maximum certificated take-off mass of more than 5,700kg; or
- certified to carry more than nineteen passengers; or
- requiring at least two pilots; or
- equipped with one or more jet engine(s) or more than one turboprop engine.

It follows that an aeroplane which doesn't meet the above criteria is an 'other-than-complex, motor-powered' aeroplane, including some surprisingly large and sophisticated aeroplanes.

A commercial operation means any operation of an aircraft in return for remuneration or other valuable consideration and is available to the public, or an operation under a contract between an operator and a customer, where the customer has no control over the operator and it is not made available to the public. It follows that, in general terms, flights which do not involve any form of remuneration or valuable consideration are 'non-commercial operations'.

The rules governing Non-Commercial Operations in 'other than complex' aircraft are contained within a set of regulations known as 'Part-NCO'. Part-NCO applies to 'Part-21' aircraft.

Figure OP2.1

Despite its size (it can carry up to nine passengers), the Pilatus PC-12 is an 'other-than-complex aircraft'.

Figure OP2.2

Another example of an 'other-than-complex aircraft'– the 11-seat Tecnam P2012 twin.

Civil Aviation Authority

CERTIFICATE OF AIRWORTHINESS

Certificate Number: **067615/001**

**United Kingdom**
**Civil Aviation Authority**

| 1. Nationality and Registration Marks | 2. Manufacturer and designation of aircraft | 3. Aircraft Serial Number |
|---|---|---|
| **G-TSFC** | **COSTRUZIONI AERONAUTICHE TECNAM SRL TECNAM P2008-JC** | **1047** |

4. Categories
**Very Light Aeroplane**

5. This Certificate of Airworthiness is issued pursuant to the Convention on International Civil Aviation dated 7 December 1944 and Regulation (EC) No 216/2008 Article 5(2)(c), in respect of the above mentioned aircraft which is considered to be airworthy when maintained and operated in accordance with the foregoing and the pertinent operating limitations.

Date of Issue: **16 April 2015** Signature:

CIVIL AVIATION AUTHORITY 123

Limitations/Remarks:
**None**

6. This Certificate of Airworthiness is valid unless revoked by the competent authority of the Member State of registry.
A current Airworthiness Review Certificate shall be attached to this Certificate.

EASA Form 25 Issue 2
**This certificate shall be carried on board during all flights**

SAMPLE

Figure OP2.3
A Certificate of Airworthiness (C of A).

'Part-21 aircraft are those which, before the UK left the European Aviation Safety Agency (EASA), had an EASA Certificate of Airworthiness. A Certificate of Airworthiness (C of A) confirms that an aircraft's design, equipment and maintenance are to an international standard.

A 'non-Part 21' aircraft is one which for some reason would not meet the criteria for an EASA certificate of airworthiness – such as many vintage, historic, ex-military, home-built and experimental aircraft. The operation of a 'non-Part 21' aircraft is governed by the Competent Authority responsible for the aircraft's registration and airworthiness, for example the UK Civil Aviation Authority (CAA) for a UK-registered aircraft.

Touring motor gliders (TMG) must be operated following the requirements for aeroplanes when they are power-driven by an engine and those for sailplanes when operated without using an engine. Powered sailplanes, (excluding TMG), must be operated and equipped in compliance with the requirements applicable to sailplanes.

The 'Part-NCO' regulation has different rules for different aircraft categories (aeroplanes, helicopters, balloons etc.) and is divided into a number of sections, including:

- General (GEN);
- Operational Procedures (OP)
- Performance and Operating Limitations (POL)
- Instruments and Equipment (IDE)

## Responsibility and authority of the Pilot-in-Command (PIC)

Within Part-NCO, the responsibilities and authority of the **Pilot-In-Command** are dealt with in some considerable detail (the Pilot-In-Command is the person designated by the owner or operator as being in command and responsible for the safe conduct of the flight).

Part-NCO states that the Pilot-In-Command (PIC) is responsible for:

- the safety of the aircraft and of all crew members, passengers and cargo on board;
- the commencement, continuation, termination or diversion of a flight in the interest of safety;
- ensuring that all operational procedures and checklists are complied with;
- only commencing a flight if he/she is satisfied that all operational limitations are complied with – including that the aircraft is airworthy, the aircraft is duly registered, the required instruments and equipment are operative, the mass and balance of the aircraft are within limits, all equipment, baggage and cargo are properly loaded and secured, an emergency evacuation remains possible, and the aircraft operating limitations will not be exceeded at any time during the flight;
- not commencing a flight if he/she is incapacitated by injury, sickness, fatigue or the effects of any psychoactive* substance;

- not continuing a flight beyond the nearest weather-permissible aerodrome or operating site when his/her capacity to perform the PIC duties is significantly degraded by causes such as fatigue, sickness or lack of oxygen;
- recording all known or suspected defects of the aircraft in the aircraft technical log or journey log for the aircraft.
- deciding whether to accept an aircraft with unserviceable items. The minimum required serviceable equipment may be listed in a Minimum Equipment List (MEL).

* A ‘psychoactive’ substance is one that has a profound or significant effect on mental processes – such as drugs and alcohol.

The Pilot-In-Command must also ensure that during critical phases of flight or whenever deemed necessary in the interest of safety, all crew members are seated at their assigned stations and do not perform any activities other than those required for the safe operation of the aircraft.

The Pilot-In-Command has the authority to refuse to carry and to disembark any person, baggage or cargo that may represent a potential hazard to the safety of the aircraft or its occupants.

Figure OP2.4
Part-NCO sets out specific responsibilities for the Pilot In Command (PIC).

The Pilot-In-Command must, as soon as possible, report to the appropriate Air Traffic Services (ATS) unit any hazardous weather or flight conditions encountered that are likely to affect the safety of other aircraft. Such hazardous conditions could include severe turbulence, severe icing, severe mountain wave, thunderstorms and wind shear.

Part-NCO also states that the Pilot-In-Command must, in an emergency situation that requires immediate decision and action, take any action he/she considers necessary under the circumstances. In such cases he/she may deviate from rules, operational procedures and methods in the interest of safety.

During flight, the Pilot-In-Command must keep his/her safety belt fastened while at his/her station; and remain at the controls of the aircraft at all times except if another pilot is taking the controls.

The Pilot-In-Command must submit a report of any act of unlawful interference, without delay, to the competent authority and the designated local authority. Additionally, the Pilot-In-Command must notify the nearest appropriate authority by the quickest available means of any accident involving the aircraft that results in serious injury or death of any person or substantial damage to the aircraft or property.

The Pilot-In-Command must comply with the laws, regulations and procedures of those States where operations are conducted. The PIC must also be familiar with the laws, regulations and procedures for the areas to be crossed, the aerodromes or operating sites to be used and related air navigation facilities. The Pilot-In-Command must only use aerodromes and operating sites that are adequate for the type of aircraft and operation planned.

Before commencing a flight, the Pilot-In-Command must check that the ground facilities required for the safe operation of the aircraft (such as communication facilities and navigation aids) are adequate for the type of operation planned.

Figure OP2.5

Before commencing a flight, the pilot-in-command must be familiar with all available meteorological information appropriate to the intended flight.

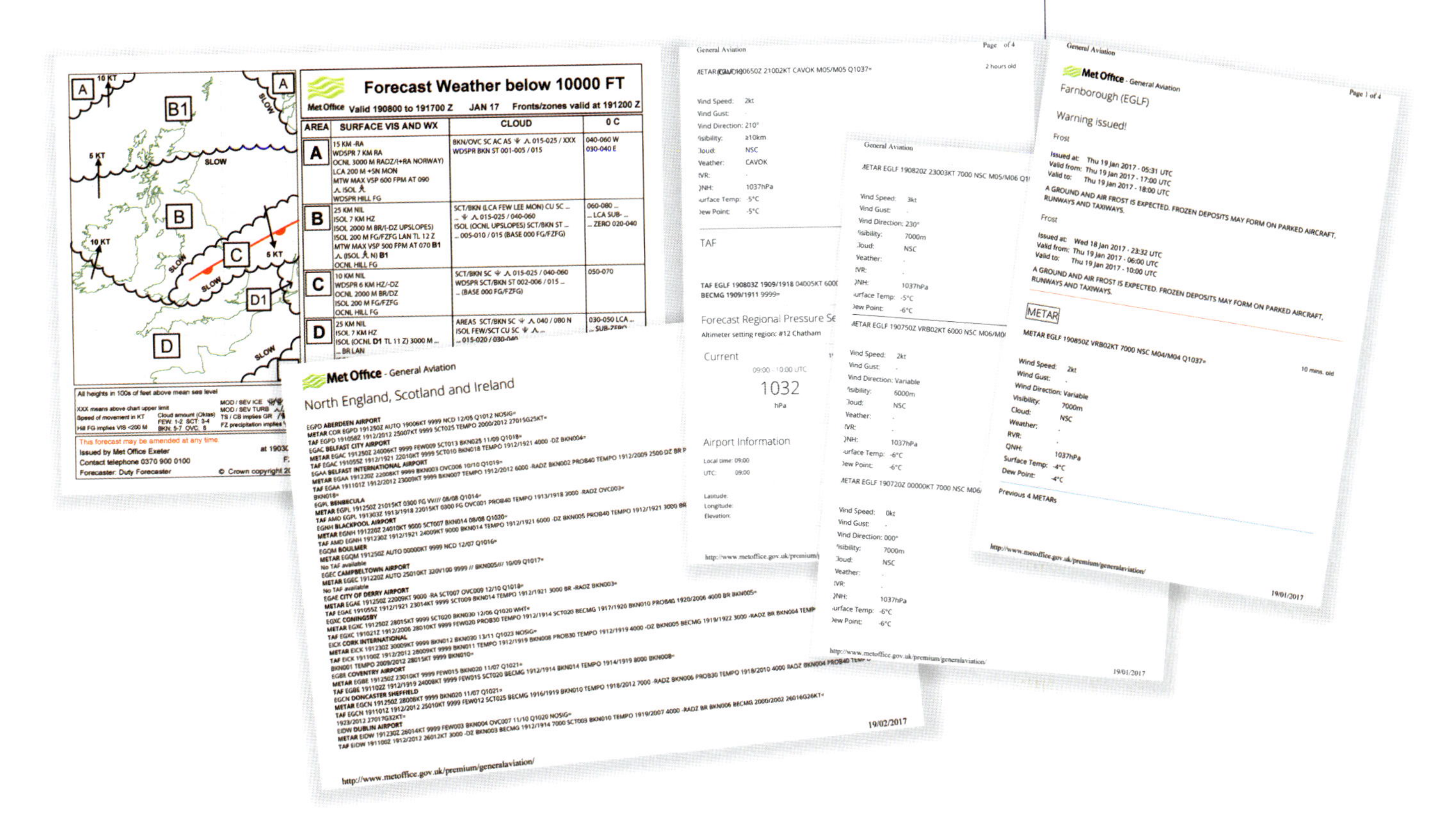

Figure OP2.6
The pilot-in-command must only continue a VFR flight if the latest available meteorological information indicates that the weather conditions will be at or above the applicable VFR minima.

Also before commencing a flight, the Pilot-In-Command must also be familiar with all available meteorological information appropriate to the intended flight. Preparation for a flight away from the vicinity of the place of departure must include a study of available current weather reports and forecasts, and planning an alternative course of action in case the flight cannot be completed as planned.

Part-NCO regulations require that the Pilot-In-Command must only commence or continue a VFR flight if the latest available meteorological information indicates that the weather conditions along the route and at the intended destination at the estimated time of use will be at or above the applicable VFR operating minima. In practical terms, this means the VMC minima.

The Pilot-In-Command must only operate the aircraft if the performance is adequate to comply with the applicable rules of the air and any other restrictions applicable to the flight, the airspace or the aerodromes or operating sites to be visited, taking into account the accuracy of any charts and maps used.

Smoking on board the aircraft shall not be allowed by the Pilot-In-Command whenever necessary in the interest of safety and during refuelling of the aircraft.

An aircraft may only commence a flight or intentionally fly into expected or actual icing conditions if the aircraft is certified and equipped for such conditions. In-flight icing is very rare in VMC flight.

Figure OP2.7
The Aircraft Flight Manual (AFM) contains essential information for the safe operation of a specific aircraft.

TECNAM P2008 JC - Aircraft Flight Manual Page 0 - 1

**Aircraft Flight Manual**
*Doc. No. 2008/100*
*Ed.1 – Rev. 0*
*2013, July 30th*

***TECNAM P2008 JC***

MANUFACTURER: COSTRUZIONI AERONAUTICHE **TECNAM** S.r.l.
AIRCRAFT MODEL: ***P2008 JC***
EASA TYPE CERTIFICATE NO: **A .583** (DATED 2013, 27TH SEPTEMBER)

SERIAL NUMBER: ........................

REGISTRATION MARKINGS: ........................

*This Aircraft Flight Manual is approved by* ***European Aviation Safety Agency (EASA)*** *and applies only EASA CS-VLA certified airplanes.*

*This Manual must be carried in the airplane at all times.*
*The airplane has to be operated in compliance with procedures and limitations contained herein.*

Costruzioni Aeronautiche **TECNAM** srl
Via Maiorise
CAPUA (CE) – Italy
Tel. +39 (0) 823 997538
WEB: www.tecnam.com

Before take-off and before landing, the Pilot-In-Command must be satisfied that the weather at the aerodrome or operating site and the condition of the runway will allow a safe take-off or landing as applicable. The latest available weather report should be used for these purposes.

Published noise abatement procedures to minimise the effect of aircraft noise at the surface must be taken into account by the PIC, although safety always has priority over noise abatement.

## Documents to be carried

Part-NCO sets out a number of documents which should be carried in an aircraft. These documents are those which relate to the airworthiness, registration and operation of the aircraft and the planned flight. The applicability and validity of various documents and certificates are an element of the safe and legal operation of an aircraft and much more than a pointless bureaucratic paperwork exercise. It follows that the pilot should be familiar with aircraft and flight documentation and the checking of this documentation is a normal part of pre-flight planning. There are several key aircraft documents:

The **Aircraft Flight Manual** (**AFM**) is a document which contains vital information on the operation of a specific aircraft including information such as limitations, operating procedures, performance

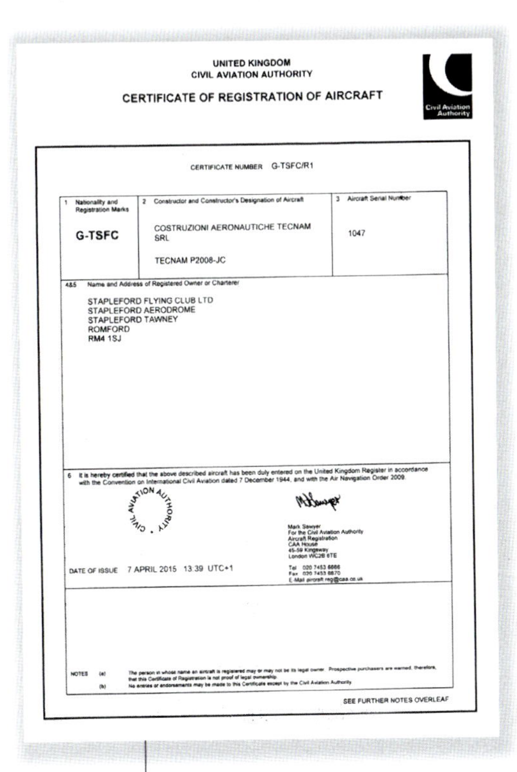

UNITED KINGDOM
CIVIL AVIATION AUTHORITY

CERTIFICATE OF REGISTRATION OF AIRCRAFT



CERTIFICATE NUMBER G-TSFC/R1

| 1 Nationality and Registration Marks | 2 Constructor and Constructor's Designation of Aircraft | 3 Aircraft Serial Number |
|---|---|---|
| G-TSFC | COSTRUZIONI AERONAUTICHE TECNAM SRL<br>TECNAM P2008-JC | 1047 |

4&5 Name and Address of Registered Owner or Charterer

STAPLEFORD FLYING CLUB LTD
STAPLEFORD AERODROME
STAPLEFORD TAWNEY
ROMFORD
RM4 1SJ

6 It is hereby certified that the above described aircraft has been duly entered on the United Kingdom Register in accordance with the Convention on International Civil Aviation dated 7 December 1944, and with the Air Navigation Order 2009.



Mark Sawyer
For the Civil Aviation Authority
Aircraft Registration
CAA House
45-59 Kingsway
London WC2B 6TE

DATE OF ISSUE 7 APRIL 2015 13:39 UTC+1

Tel 020 7453 6666
Fax 020 7453 6670
E-Mail aircraft.reg@caa.co.uk

NOTES (a) The person in whose name an aircraft is registered may or may not be its legal owner. Prospective purchasers are warned, therefore, that this Certificate of Registration is not proof of legal ownership.
(b) No entries or endorsements may be made to this Certificate except by the Civil Aviation Authority.

SEE FURTHER NOTES OVERLEAF

Figure OP2.8
A Certificate of Registration (C of R) confirms the registration marks allocated to an aircraft and the aircraft ownership.

data, checklists etc. An individual aircraft will have its own individual AFM, annotated as belonging to a specific aircraft and amended and updated as necessary if the aircraft's equipment changes or operating experience shows that a revision of the AFM is necessary.

A **Certificate of Registration** (**C of R**) confirms the registration marks allocated to an aircraft and the aircraft ownership. It also confirms the 'state of registry' of an aircraft, which may affect the regulations applicable to it, and confirms the exact type and mark of the aircraft.

A **Certificate of Airworthiness** (**C of A**), confirms that the aircraft is designed and maintained to an internationally-recognised standard. A C of A may state specific limitations on the operation of the aircraft, or may be restricted in some way. If an aircraft type is not eligible for the issue of a C of A, aircraft may instead be issued with a 'Permit to Fly'. A **Permit to Fly** will normally restrict the operation of an aircraft in some way (for example the flight conditions it may or may not operate in), compared to an aircraft with a C of A.

An aircraft may be required to have a Noise Certificate which may state the external noise level of the aircraft both for 'overflight' and during take-off. The requirement for a noise certificates varies between different states.

If the aircraft is fitted with radios, it may be required to have an aircraft Radio Licence, essentially a permission to operate the radios fitted in the aircraft. It may be necessary to pay a regular fee maintain the validity of the aircraft radio licence.

A journey log (or logbook) contains information about each flight an aircraft makes including dates, flight crew, places of departure and arrival, flight times, any incidents and observations and the signature of the PIC. The journey log may take the form of an aircraft 'technical log'.

Figure OP2.9
An aircraft 'technical log'.

G-XXXX TECH LOG Sheet No......

N85LB Defects and Rectification log Sheet No ...........

| rial | Date | Defect details | Pilot initials | Rectification / follow up | Signature | Date |
|---|---|---|---|---|---|---|

G-XXXX TECH LOG Sheet No......

| Ref No | Date | Start Fuel (L) | Oil Add | Pilot | Passenger | Exercise/Route | Brakes Off (UTC) | Brakes On (UTC) | Total | End Fuel (est) L | Fuel Uplift (L) | New Defect | Flight Time | Hours to next check |
|---|---|---|---|---|---|---|---|---|---|---|---|---|---|---|



Figure OP2.10
An aircraft's 'Minimum Equipment List' (MEL).

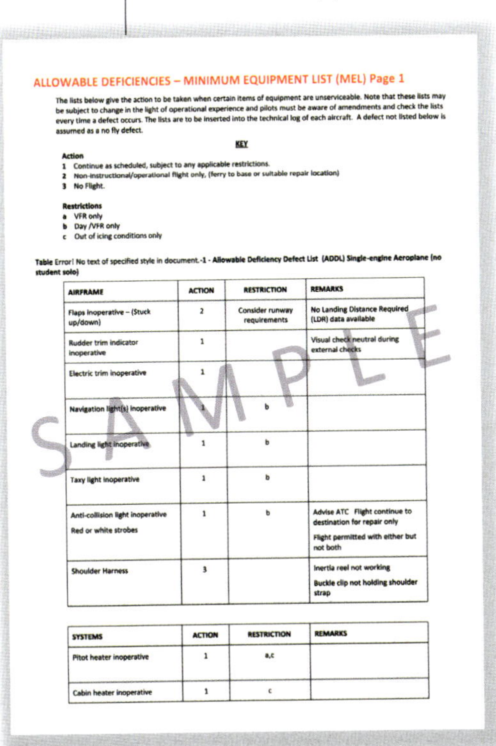

ALLOWABLE DEFICIENCIES – MINIMUM EQUIPMENT LIST (MEL) Page 1

The lists below give the action to be taken when certain items of equipment are unserviceable. Note that these lists may be subject to change in the light of operational experience and pilots must be aware of amendments and check the lists every time a defect occurs. The lists are to be inserted into the technical log of each aircraft. A defect not listed below is assumed as a no fly defect.

KEY

**Action**
1 Continue as scheduled, subject to any applicable restrictions.
2 Non-instructional/operational flight only, (ferry to base or suitable repair location)
3 No Flight.

**Restrictions**
a VFR only
b Day /VFR only
c Out of icing conditions only

**Table** Error! No text of specified style in document.-1 - **Allowable Deficiency Defect List (ADDL) Single-engine Aeroplane (no student solo)**

| AIRFRAME | ACTION | RESTRICTION | REMARKS |
|---|---|---|---|
| Flaps inoperative – (Stuck up/down) | 2 | Consider runway requirements | No Landing Distance Required (LDR) data available |
| Rudder trim indicator inoperative | 1 | | Visual check neutral during external checks |
| Electric trim inoperative | 1 | | |
| Navigation light(s) inoperative | 1 | b | |
| Landing light inoperative | 1 | b | |
| Taxy light inoperative | 1 | b | |
| Anti-collision light inoperative<br>Red or white strobes | 1 | b | Advise ATC Flight continue to destination for repair only<br>Flight permitted with either but not both |
| Shoulder Harness | 3 | | Inertia reel not working<br>Buckle clip not holding shoulder strap |

| SYSTEMS | ACTION | RESTRICTION | REMARKS |
|---|---|---|---|
| Pitot heater inoperative | 1 | a,c | |
| Cabin heater inoperative | 1 | c | |

An aircraft may have a **Minimum Equipment List** (**MEL**) which is, as the name implies, a document listing the minimum aircraft equipment required for flight under various conditions, and procedures for dealing with equipment unserviceability.

According to part-NCO, the following documentation must be carried in an aircraft during flight (copies of documentation are acceptable except where stated):

- The original Certificate of Registration;
- The original Certificate of Airworthiness or Permit to Fly;
- The Noise Certificate (if applicable)
- The aircraft Radio Licence (if applicable);
- The Insurance Certificate;
- The Journey Log or equivalent (such as a 'technical log');
- A list of specific approvals, if applicable.

If a flight is planned to take-off and land at the same place, or if the flight is planned to remain within a distance or area specified by the Competent Authority, it may be permissible to retain the above documentation at the place of departure.

Regardless of the requirement to carry (or not carry) the above documents, Part-NCO states that the following additional documentation must be carried on every flight:

- The Aircraft Flight Manual (AFM) or equivalent;
- The Minimum Equipment List (MEL) if applicable;
- Details of any Air Traffic Services (ATS) flight plan filed;
- Current and suitable aeronautical charts for the planned route including reasonable diversion routes;
- Information on procedures and signals regarding aircraft interception;
- Any other information relevant to the flight or required by the State(s) concerned with the flight.

To be 'suitable', the aeronautical charts carried should contain data appropriate to the applicable air traffic regulations, rules of the air, flight altitudes, the area/route and nature of the operation. Aeronautical data on the chart should include airspace structure; navigation aids (navaids) and air traffic services (ATS) routes; navigation and communication frequencies; prohibited, restricted and danger areas; other sites that may hazard the flight; and topographical data including terrain and obstacles.

Except where original documentation is specified, documents, manuals and information do not have to be 'hard copies' printed on paper. Electronic storage of documents is acceptable if the pilot is satisfied that accessibility, usability and reliability can be guaranteed.

In accordance with Flight Crew Licencing (Part-FCL) requirements, a valid licence and a valid medical certificate must be carried by the pilot, together with some form of 'personal identification document' containing his/her photo.

If the Competent Authority requires it, the Pilot-in-Command must produce any documentation that a flight is required to carry within 'a reasonable time' of being requested to do so.

## Dangerous goods

According to ICAO, **dangerous goods** are articles or substances capable of posing a significant risk to health, safety or property when transported by air. There are many items and substances which, while perfectly safe for surface transport, can represent a serious safety hazard if loaded onto an aircraft. Commercial aviation operations, in particular passenger and cargo transport, are subject to strict rules regarding dangerous goods, with severe penalties for companies or individuals who break these rules – whether intentionally or by negligence.

For non-commercial, General Aviation (GA) operations, the greatest danger from 'dangerous goods' comes from items that pilots or passengers may bring onto an aircraft without realising the hazard they represent. Part-NCO requires that the Pilot-In-Command (PIC) must take all reasonable measures to prevent dangerous goods being bought onto an aircraft inadvertently, and must also provide passengers with information about dangerous goods.

Some goods are self-evidently dangerous on or off an aircraft – for example explosives, ammunition, firearms, large knives or other weapons. As a general rule items of this sort should be considered as forbidden on an aircraft. Other 'dangerous goods' which are not usually allowed on an aircraft include:

- Camping stoves that run on flammable liquid or gas;
- Diving cylinders pressurised to over 2.8bar (40psi);
- Fireworks;
- Flammable paint (although water-based and artist paints are permissible);
- Lighter fuel and lighter refills;
- Party Poppers;
- Smoke hood with oxygen supply;
- 'Strike anywhere' matches;
- Oxidisers (such as those used in kitchen cleaners).

Figure OP2.11
Some examples of dangerous goods which should not be taken on board an aircraft, from a UK CAA Safety Poster.

Figure OP2.12
This chainsaw and the fuel canister also represent good examples of 'dangerous goods', the carriage of which in an aircraft requires serious consideration at the very least.

Figure OP2.13
This camping stove, with attached gas cylinder, would be classified as 'dangerous goods' in an aircraft.

Other items which should be considered as dangerous on an aircraft include acids and other corrosive liquids, thinners, poisons, weed killers and insecticides, gas containers, radioactive materials, mercury barometers and batteries. For items that might be found inside baggage, such as aerosols, batteries, toiletries, heated hair curlers etc. the best approach is to check the current advice for airline passengers and use that as a guide when deciding what to allow on board the aircraft.

Figure OP2.14
Globally Harmonised System (GHS) pictograms.

**GHS Pictograms**

Flame (Flammables)
Flame Over Circle (Oxidizers)
Exploding Bomb (Explosives)
Corrosive (Corrosives)
Gas Cylinder (Gases Under Pressure)
Skull & Crossbones (Acute Toxicity)
Exclamation Mark (Irritants/Sensitizers/ Other Hazards)
Environment (Aquatic Hazards)
Health Hazard (Specific Toxicity Hazards)

Pictured are the standard hazard symbols used in the GHS. Symbols can be used individually and in combinations to define the specific hazard(s) of the chemical.

Chemicals and other potentially hazardous goods may carry consumer labelling in according with Globally Harmonised System (GHS) classifications. Certain labels indicate that the item should be considered as hazardous or dangerous, (although not if the wording in the danger and hazard description refers only to 'serious eye damage').

In a small aircraft any baggage and items bought on board by passengers will be much closer to the cockpit equipment and instrumentation than in an airliner, and these can represent specific risks in small aircraft. Magnetic materials may affect the compass reading if placed too close to the compass – and magnets are used in a wide range of consumer products including toys, speakers, computers, hand-held electronic devices, mobile phones etc. In most aircraft the compass is mounted on or above the instrument panel and so care must be taken to avoid placing potentially magnetic items close to the compass (for example, on the 'coaming' above or around the instrument panel). The mounting devices for portable devices may also generate a magnetic field which can alter the compass reading. The growth in the number of portable electronic devices regularly carried around by many pilots, and use of such devices to run aviation-specific applications, makes the magnetic hazard a very real consideration in the cockpit of a light aircraft.

Figure OP2.15
Objects containing magnetic materials must not be placed near the compass. In this example, a portable speaker placed near the compass has deflected the reading by almost 180 degrees.

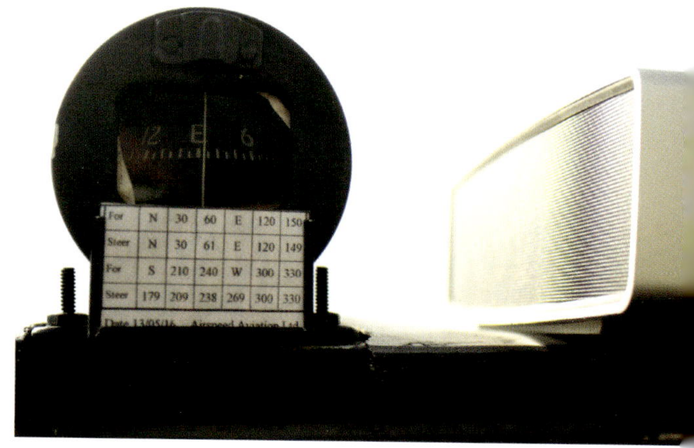

There are some substances – for example spare oil, de-icing fluid or spare batteries, which could be considered to be 'dangerous goods' but are also sometimes necessary or advisable to carry in an aircraft. To cater for this legal nicety, Part-NCO states, *"Reasonable quantities of articles and substances that would otherwise be classified as dangerous goods and that are used to facilitate flight safety, shall be considered authorised .... The packing and loading on board of the these articles and substances shall be performed under the responsibility of the Pilot-In-Command, in such a way as to minimise the risks posed to crew members, passengers, cargo or the aircraft during aircraft operations."*

In addition to the magnetic hazard, **Portable Electronic Devices** (**PED**) can have other adverse effects on cockpit instrumentation. PEDs are any kind of electronic device (typically, but not limited to, consumer electronics), brought on board the aircraft. Even PEDs which are not equipped with a transmitting function can radiate transmissions and such PEDs can include calculators, cameras, radios, audio and video players, electronic games and toys etc. The transmissions these devices can radiate may have an undetermined effect on aircraft instrumentation and avionics. PEDs which do have an intentional transmitting function can include two-way radios, mobile phones and computers with mobile data connection and/or Bluetooth and/or wireless local area network (WLAN) capability. Even when such PEDs are set to 'flight mode' they may still radiate in some way.

Figure OP2.16
Portable Electronic Devices (PED) can be exceptionally useful in aviation, but their use in and around aircraft does need careful consideration.

Another risk posed by PEDs comes from the batteries that power them, in particular the lithium batteries increasingly used in PEDs. Modern batteries may be very efficient, but they are also occasionally subject to a condition called 'thermal runaway', which can lead the batteries in a device to over-heat and burst into flames. An FAA study found that 158 serious in-flight incidents had occurred involving batteries in a 25-year period, and airlines ban spare lithium batteries from hold luggage. The FAA recommend that any spare lithium batteries must be individually protected to prevent short circuits (eg by keeping them in their original packaging, or insulating the terminals by taping over exposed terminals, or placing each battery in a separate plastic bag or protective pouch). The FAA also recommend that spare batteries must not come in contact with metal objects, such as coins, keys, or jewellery etc., and steps should be taken to prevent crushing, puncturing, or pressure on the battery. For all these reasons, it is sensible to make sure that any PEDs and spare batteries carried in a light aircraft, even those not in use, are placed where they are readily accessible by the occupants in the event of a problem such as thermal runway.

Increasingly airlines are allowing the use of PEDs by passengers on board and in-flight, including those with intentional transmitting functions, but they can only do so once they have proved to the aviation authorities that such use will not adversely affect the aircraft's instrumentation. The detailed studies and evidence required to obtain such permission, and the average distance of such devices from the cockpit in the typical airliner, is very different to the situation in a General Aviation aircraft. Whilst it may be unrealistic to ban PEDs from the cockpit of a light aircraft, there is no doubt that the in-flight use of any PED must be carefully considered beforehand. Anytime a PED is in use, the pilot should be alert to any interference with aircraft systems and be ready to turn off such devices if there is any suspicion that interference is occurring. Part-NCO is quite clear on the use of PEDs in an aircraft: *"The Pilot-In-Command shall not permit any person to use a Portable Electronic Device (PED) on board an aircraft that could adversely affect the performance of the aircraft's systems and equipment."*

The use of mobile phones in flight is a source of considerable and continuing debate amongst pilots. It is generally agreed that for VFR flight, the potential interference with radio navigation equipment, for example, should not present a serious hazard. Furthermore, whilst it is theoretically possible for a mobile phone (or other PED) to interfere with electronic flight displays in the cockpit, instances of this actually occurring in service seem to be rare. Once again, the best advice is to proceed with caution and be alert to possible disruption of cockpit displays or radios by PEDs and if they are not required for the conduct of the flight, simply switch off any PEDs.

Other hazards posed by PEDs may be less obvious. It is widely believed (although difficult to prove) that using a mobile phone in flight may disrupt the ground-based mobile phone networks which are, after-all, designed for surface-based phones travelling relatively slowly. It has been also reported on aviation forums that pilots who have disrupted a mobile phone network by using their mobile phones in-flight have had their phones cut-off or barred from the network as a result. However, the greatest risk posed by the use of PEDs in the cockpit may have nothing to do with their physical properties.

Numerous studies of driving behaviour have shown that the use of mobile phones whilst driving causes a significant distraction to the driver, with consequent increase in poor driving standards and risk of accident (even when a 'hands free' device is being used). A recent study in the USA has claimed that 18% of all fatal road accidents are caused by mobile phone use. The most blatant examples of distraction include drivers

Figure OP2.17
Texting whilst driving or flying an aeroplane is exceptionally dangerous – not surprisingly both actions have led to a number of fatal accidents.

checking e-mails, social media and even reading and sending text messages whilst driving. Not surprisingly, this last behaviour in particular has led to a significant number of fatal accidents. Unfortunately this trend has spread to aviation and investigations into some fatal aviation accidents have uncovered evidence of the pilots involved reading and sending text messages in the moments before the accident. Even if the accident itself was not directly related to the action of texting, it is only common sense that such distraction from the pilot's primary task (that of flying the aircraft) must be considered as a significant contributory factor. The risks associated with the use of PEDs in-flight for activities not related to the flight are sufficiently serious that the American Federal Aviation Authority (FAA) have banned the use of PEDs for personal use in flight by airline crews. It follows that in the normal 'single crew' operation of a General Aviation aircraft, the personal use of PEDs (such as texting) can only be a distraction and a serious flight hazard. The business of safely operating an aircraft is one that demands the full attention of the pilot. Anything that diverts the pilot's attention away from the job of operating the aircraft is an unnecessary flight safety hazard. For many pilots, one of the attractions of flying is the immersion in a different environment where normal day-to-day frustrations and distractions can be left behind for a while. Allowing those distractions back into the cockpit is a retrograde step that can have no flight safety benefit.

*"Call logs for the phone indicated that the pilot had been making and receiving voice calls during the accident flight and that he had sent an SMS text message from the same phone several minutes before the aircraft crashed."*

*"The pilot sent five text messages and received five text messages during the 25 minute flight. These messages...were used to exchange information, some of which the pilot appeared to have used to make operational decisions. The CAA acknowledges the utility of mobile phones but is concerned that they can distract pilots from their primary role and should not be used except in an emergency."*

Figure OP2.18
Extracts from two fatal accident reports by the UK Air Accidents Investigation Branch (AAIB).

## Fuel and oil, refuelling

It is only common sense that a flight will proceed more smoothly and efficiently if the aircraft has more than enough fuel and oil on board, and if that fuel and oil is of the correct grades. It should also not come as a surprise that regardless of other circumstances, the responsibility for ensuring that the aircraft always has enough fuel and oil always rests with the Pilot-In-Command (PIC).

Under Part-NCO, absolute **minimum fuel reserves** are set down for a VFR flight, for a day-time VFR flight these minimums are:

- When taking-off and landing at the same aerodrome or landing site, and always remaining in sight of that aerodrome or landing site: sufficient fuel and oil to fly the intended route with a reserve of at least 10 minutes at normal cruising altitude.
- In all other circumstances: sufficient fuel and oil to fly to the aerodrome of intended landing with a reserve of at least 30 minutes at normal cruising altitude.

The detailed calculation of fuel required is covered elsewhere, however it is fair to say that most pilots will want to land with considerable more fuel left in the tanks than these legal minimums. Nevertheless, Part-NCO also places a duty on the Pilot-In-Command to check at regular intervals in flight that the amount of usable fuel remaining is not less than the fuel required to proceed to a weather-permissible aerodrome or operating site, plus the planned reserve fuel.

Once the required fuel load has been calculated, deciding what type of fuel or oil to put into the aircraft is not as simple a process as it might be in a car, for example.

The key reference document for **fuel grades** is the Aircraft Flight Manual (AFM) for the actual aircraft to be flown. The AFM will state the acceptable fuel types and grades, however developments in fuel grades since many General Aviation aircraft were first designed may mean that additional fuel types of grades can be used if the engine manufacturer permits it.

**Cirrus Design**
**SR22**

**Section 1**
**General**

**Fuel**

Total Capacity ............ 84.0 U.S. Gallons (318.0 L)
Total Usable ............ 81.0 U.S. Gallons (306.6 L)
Approved Fuel Grades:
100 LL Grade Aviation Fuel (Blue)
100 (Formerly 100/130) Grade Aviation Fuel (Green)

**Oil**

Oil Capacity (Sump) ............ 8 U.S. Quarts (7.6 L)
Oil Grades:
All Temperatures ............ SAE 15W-50, 20W-50, or 20W-60
Below 40 °F (4° C) ............ SAE 30
Above 40 °F (4° C) ............ SAE 50

Figure OP2.19
An extract from an Aircraft Flight Manual showing the approved fuel and oil grades.

**Table 3**
**Fuels Approved for Use in Lycoming Engine Models**

| Engine Models | Leaded Aviation Fuels (Table 1) | | | | Unleaded Aviation Fuels (Table 1) | | Unleaded Automotive Fuels (Table 2) | | |
|---|---|---|---|---|---|---|---|---|---|
| | ASTM D910 | TU 38 | GOST 1012 | | ASTM D7547 | HJELMCO | ASTM D4814 | | EN228 |
| | 100* 100LL 100VLL | 91* | B91/115* | B95/130* | UL 91 | 91/96 | 91 AKI | 93 AKI | NB.3 |
| **O-235** | | | | | | | | | |
| -C, -E, -H | ● | ● | ● | ● | ● | ● | | ● | ● |
| -F, -G, -J | ● | | | ● | | | | | |
| -K, -L, -N | ● | | | ● | ● | | | ● | ● |
| -M, -P | ● | | | | ● | | | ● | ● |
| **O-290** | | | | | | | | | |
| -D | ● | ● | ● | ● | ● | ● | | ● | ● |
| **O-320** | | | | | | | | | |
| -A, -B, -C, -D, -E | ● | ● | ● | ● | ● | ● | | ● | ● |
| -H | ● | | | | | | | | |
| **IO-320** | | | | | | | | | |
| -A, -B, -D, -E | ● | ● | ● | ● | ● | ● | | ● | ● |
| -C, -F | ● | | | ● | | | | | |
| **AIO-320** | | | | | | | | | |
| -A, -B, -C | ● | ● | ● | ● | ● | ● | | ● | ● |
| **LIO-320** | | | | | | | | | |
| -B | ● | ● | ● | ● | ● | ● | | ● | ● |
| -C | ● | | | ● | | | | | |
| **AEIO-320** | | | | | | | | | |
| -D | ● | ● | ● | ● | | ● | | | |
| -E | ● | ● | ● | ● | ● | ● | | | |
| **O-360** | | | | | | | | | |
| -A, -B, -C, -D, -F, -G, -J | ● | ● | ● | ● | ● | ● | | ● | ● |
| -E | ● | | | | | | | | |

| ISSUED | | | REVISED | | | PAGE NO. | REVISION | |
|---|---|---|---|---|---|---|---|---|
| MO | DAY | YEAR | MO | DAY | YEAR | | | |
| 11 | 09 | 62 | 04 | 24 | 13 | 6 of 11 | S | S.I. 1070 |

Figure OP2.20
An extract from an engine manufacturer's Service Instruction regarding approved fuel grades for different engine models.

Arguably the most common type of aviation fuel for General Aviation aircraft is an aviation-specific type of petrol known as **AVGAS** (**Av**iation **GAS**oline). AVGAS is absolutely not the same as the petrol used by most cars, it has properties and additives specific to aero engines and is usually subject to detailed storage and dispensing procedures. AVGAS is available in different grades, the most common of which is '100LL'. For various reasons the production of AVGAS 100LL is being gradually phased out and so alternative AVGAS fuel grades may be found at airfields, the most common of these alternatives is AVGAS 91UL. AVGAS 91UL is NOT approved for use in all aircraft engines that can use 100LL and it is the pilot's responsibility to check if the use of 91UL is acceptable in the aircraft/engine combination. Because 91UL has come into use in the time since many GA aircraft were designed, it may be necessary to check for amendments to the aircraft's AFM regarding fuel grades. If information cannot be found in the AFM, the engine manufacturer may issue information (often in the form of a 'Service Letter', 'Service Bulletin' or 'Service Instruction') regarding acceptable fuel grades and operating instructions. Those instructions may include the use of specific oil grades when using specific fuel grades. Because many popular GA aircraft and engine designs have been in production for many years, it is not uncommon that an aircraft type may have be approved for certain fuel grades if equipped with one engine model, but not with another. This makes it all the more important to check the situation against authoritative documents and not rely on anecdotal evidence or 'word of mouth' information when deciding what fuel grade to use.

Many (but not all) aero engines which are approved to use AVGAS can also use 'normal' automotive petrol, known as MOGAS (**MO**tor **GAS**oline). As with the use of alternative AVGAS grades, the use of MOGAS must permitted in the aircraft's AFM and/or the engine manufacturer's published information and such use may be subject to specific limitations and procedures. The most common issue regarding MOGAS is the requirement to use MOGAS which meets a very specific standard. MOGAS may contain quantities of methanol and ethanol which could be harmful to aero engines and aircraft fuel systems. For that reason, it is common for the aircraft and/or engine manufacture to specify that MOGAS to be used in an aircraft must meet a European standard known as EN228. If MOGAS is dispensed from an airfield installation is it likely that this specification has been checked. However, if obtaining MOGAS from a non-aviation source (such as an automotive petrol

Figure OP2.21
All aircraft refuelling points should have notices stating the acceptable fuel type – in these examples the approved fuel is AVGAS 100LL.

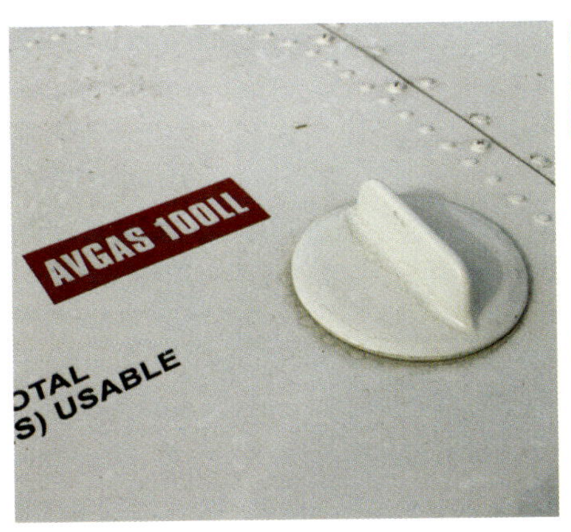

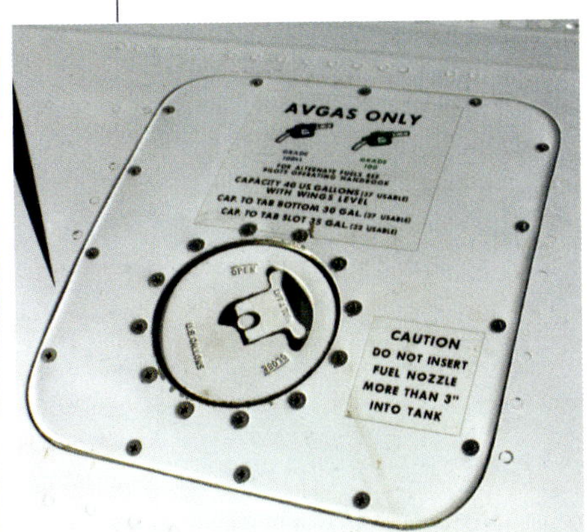

Figure OP2.22
A refuelling tanker dispensing AVGAS UL91

Figure OP2.23
An aircraft which can be fuelled with either MOGAS meeting a certain specification, or AVGAS 100LL.

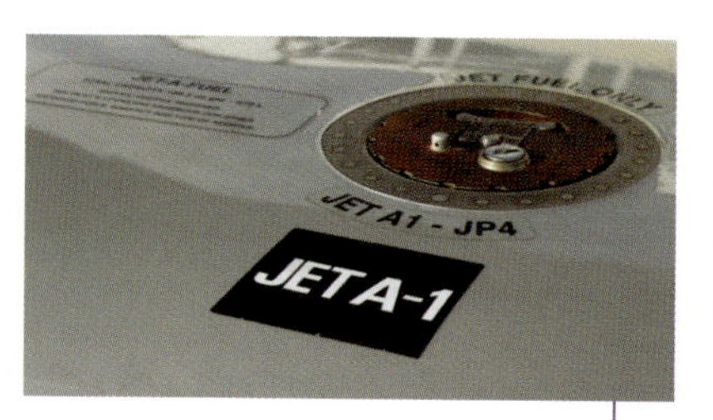


Figure OP2.24
A notice at the re-fuelling point of an aircraft which requires JET A-1 fuel.

station) the pilot may need to make detailed enquiries to ensure the required grade and standard of MOGAS is being obtained. It is a point of debate amongst pilots and engineers as to whether an average petrol station stores and dispenses MOGAS to the same standards as an aviation installation. It is commonly believed, although not necessarily proven, that an average non-aviation MOGAS installation dispenses a poorer quality product than that from an aviation installation. Some precautions suggested if obtaining MOGAS from a non-aviation installation include using a busy petrol station, where MOGAS is less likely to have been sitting in storage tanks for extended periods.

A third type of aviation fuel, increasingly used in General Aviation, is **JET A-1**. JET A-1 is used in jet engines as the name implies, but is also suitable for use in the 'diesel' type engines now found in many General Aviation aircraft. The situation regarding AVGAS/MOGAS engines and JET A-1 engines is rather like that for petrol and diesel cars – using the wrong type of fuel is likely to lead to catastrophic engine damage and probable engine failure in a very short period of time. The situation is complicated by the fact that there are several GA aircraft types which are available with either AVGAS/MOGAS engines or JET A-1 engines. It is also increasingly common to 'retrofit' an aircraft with a JET A-1-fuelled engine for economic reasons. The problem is that in an average GA aircraft, both engine types drive a propeller and so it may not be immediately obvious what type of engine is fitted to an aircraft and what type of fuel it requires.

To guard against accidentally refuelling with the wrong type of fuel, the refuelling point(s) on an aircraft should have notices which specify the permitted fuel type (eg 'AVGAS'; 'JET A-1'). Indeed, some airports take the issue of potential mis-fuelling so seriously that refuelling staff may refuse to refuel an aircraft with any fuel type or grade other than that specified on an external notice next to the aircraft's refuelling point.

As with fuel types, the primary source of information regarding permitted **oil types and grades** is the aircraft's AFM, backed-up by published information from the engine manufacturer. Also in common with fuel grades, aero engines often require oil types different to those used in car engines. AVGAS/MOGAS engines use different oil types to 'diesel' engines, and 'two-stroke' engines are likely to use different oil to that for more common 'four-stroke' engines. From this it should be obvious that the oil type to be used in an aircraft engine requires rather more consideration than simply finding the nearest bottle of oil and pouring it straight into the engine.

Aviation oils for use in AVGAS/MOGAS engines are generally of two types, 'Straight Mineral' Oil and 'Ashless Dispersant' Oil.

| Oil Type | Useage | Designation |
|---|---|---|
| Straight Mineral Oil | This type of oil is sometimes used for 'running-in' a new engine and for use when an engine has had a major overhaul or component repair. | Commercial grade only, eg '80', '100' etc. |
| Ashless Dispersant Oil | This type of oil is generally used in 'normal' service when the use of 'straight' oil is not required. | Commercial grade with prefix, eg 'W100', 'D80' etc. |

Figure OP2.25
A guide to aircraft oil grades

The aircraft AFM may specify the permitted oil in terms of an 'SAE' grade (with different recommended SAE grades dependant on the average air temperature when starting). However – unhelpfully – aviation oil is sold and packaged using commercial grades, which may be different. In general terms a lower commercial grade is used for lower air temperature conditions and in practice only grades 80 and 100 are widely available in Europe.

Aviation oil may also be available as a 'multi-grade' – for example '20W-50' or 'W15W50'.

Different oil types, with different designations, are usually required for 'diesel' aero engines which use JET A-1 fuel.

If an engine is fitted with a gearbox, the aircraft and engine manufacturer will specify the oil to be used in the gearbox.

Figure OP2.26
A typical re-fuelling installation at a General Aviation (GA) airfield.

Figure OP2.27
A safety notice on an airfield re-fuelling installation.

The **refuelling of an aircraft** is a very routine operation, but one that is noticeably more complex than the process of fuelling a car, for example. Any potential source of ignition is a risk during refuelling; some sources are obvious – such as matches or lighters, open flames, tools producing sparks, lit cigarettes etc and these are banned from being near to any refuelling installation (typically no closer than 20 metres).

Figure OP2.28
Some typical fuel-type notices on airfield re-fuelling installations.

Figure OP2.29
A bonding wire with clip on an airfield re-fuelling installation.

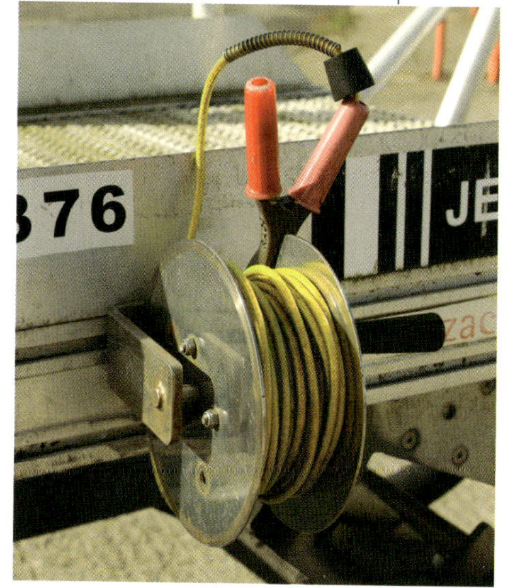

A less obvious risk comes from the possible discharge of static electricity in the form of a spark – clearly a very dangerous occurrence during refuelling. Static electricity may be created when two differing surfaces rub or pass by each other. This may lead a poorly conducting surface to build up a static electricity charge and if this charge becomes large enough compared to that around it, static electricity may 'discharge' in the form of a spark. Aircraft are quite susceptible to building-up static electricity (which is why they tend to have 'static wicks' along trailing edges to dissipate static electricity charge into the atmosphere). The process of refuelling itself may also build-up static electricity as fuel pours into the aircraft tanks under pressure. To minimise the danger of static electricity discharge, the fuelling installation should be 'bonded' to the aircraft with a electricity-conducting wire before re-fuelling begins, so that there is little if any difference in electrical charge between the fuelling installation and the aircraft, making an electrical discharge (such as a spark) less likely. The bonding wire is usually in the form of a metallic wire which is attached to the fuelling installation at one end. At the other end of the wire is a metal clip and this clip is attached onto some metallic (not plastic or painted) section of the aircraft before refuelling begins – commonly a non-painted metal section of the undercarriage or an exhaust pipe.

The use of mobile phones and other PEDs is usually banned during aircraft refuelling, because even if the risk of the PED generating a spark is low, the risk of distraction from the task in hand is very high.

Many of the basic precautions to be taken when refuelling an aircraft are nothing more than common sense, with some additional aviation-specific considerations. Nevertheless, it is worth repeating that regardless of who is actually doing the refuelling process, the safety of the aircraft and the responsibility for making sure the correct fuel is loaded in the aircraft always rests with the Pilot-In-Command (PIC).

Figure OP2.30
Refuelling an aircraft, note the bonding wire attached to the aircraft exhaust.

Figure OP2.31
Another view of the bonding wire attached to the aircraft exhaust.

Figure OP2.32
Check that fire extinguishers are available at or near the fuel installation before re-fuelling an aircraft.

**Before Refuelling**

- Check what grade of fuel is required, double check against notices at the aircraft re-fuelling points.
- Ensure that the fuel installation will dispense the correct grade of fuel, based on the signage on the installation.
- Do not refuel an aircraft inside a hangar.
- If taxiing to the installation, position the aircraft parallel to, or alongside, the installation rather than 'head on' to it (in case of brake failure).
- The aircraft should be fully shut down (engine and electrical system) before AVGAS/MOGAS refuelling begins.
- The 'bonding wire' must be attached to the aircraft before refuelling begins.
- Refuelling with AVGAS or a 'wide-cut' fuel* is not allowed under Part-NCO when passengers are on-board, embarking or disembarking an aircraft.
- If passengers are permitted on-board (for example if refuelling with JET A-1), Part-NCO requires that the aircraft is manned by suitably qualified personnel ready to direct an evacuation if necessary.
- Check the availability of fire extinguishers on or near the refuelling installation.
- Do not allow naked flames, matches, lighters, lit cigarettes, spark-producing tools or use of PEDs near the refuelling installation.
- Do not refuel if a thunderstorm is near, due to the risk from lightning.

*a 'wide-cut fuel' is generally taken to be a specific blend of JET-type fuel, only used in extremely cold climates.

Figure OP2.33
High-wing aircraft may require a ladder or steps to be used for re-fuelling, in which case the usual safety precautions apply. Obviously.

**During Refuelling**

- If a ladder or similar is needed (eg for a high-wing aircraft), exercise the usual common-sense precautions.
- Do not allow the fuel nozzle to become contaminated – for example by letting it fall onto the ground.
- Position the nozzle deep into the fuel tank to avoid splash back.
- Check the fuel colour as it flows into the tank: AVGAS 100LL is light blue, JET A-1 is usually clear and each has a distinctive smell.
- Avoid contact with fuel. If any does get onto the skin, wash it off without delay. If ingested or splashed into eyes, seek medical attention.

- Monitor the fuel level in the tank to avoid over-filling, report any spillages immediately.
- Re-fit the aircraft fuel caps securely.

**After Refuelling**

- Stow the fuel nozzle carefully to avoid contamination, reel in the fuel hose if necessary.
- Remember to detach the bonding wire!
- Collect any re-fuelling documentation as necessary.
- If other aircraft are waiting for refuelling, be considerate and move off the refuelling area without undue delay.

If refuelling from drums or other canisters, additional precautions apply. Where at all possible use metal fuel containers and funnels, the use of plastic fuel containers is generally discouraged. If possible, use a conductive wire to electrically 'bond' the fuel container and aircraft before refuelling. If the funnel does not have a built-in filter, a chamois leather filter can be used.

## Instruments and equipment

Part-NCO specifies **minimum aircraft instruments and equipment** for flight although, as you might expect, most aircraft have far more instruments and equipment than the legal minimum required.

For daytime VFR flight, an aircraft is required to have at least the means of measuring and displaying the following:

- Magnetic direction;
- Altitude;
- Indicated airspeed;
- Time in hours, minutes and seconds.

Figure OP2.34
This Tiger Moth cockpit only requires the pilot to supply an accurate time piece to meet the minimum instrumentation required by EASA for VFR flight.

Instruments and equipment installed in an aircraft, and those used to control the aircraft's flightpath, must be of a type approved in accordance with airworthiness requirements. Flight is not permitted if any of the required instruments or equipment are inoperative or missing, unless the aircraft is operated in accordance with a Minimum Equipment List (MEL) or the aircraft has a valid Permit to Fly.

The instrumentation required for basic VFR flight is traditionally provided in the form of 'round dial' instrumentation.

Magnetic direction is usually displayed on a compass. Altitude is displayed on an altimeter which is calibrated in feet, with a 'sub scale' adjustment so that pressure in millibars or hectopascals can be set. Airspeed can be displayed on an Airspeed Indicator (ASI), which usually displays airspeed in 'knots', although if the aircraft has a maximum take-off weight below 2000kg, it may display in miles per hour (MPH) or kilometres per hour (KPH) if those units are used in the Aircraft Flight Manual (AFM).

Figure OP2.35
A seat belt with shoulder strap in a light aircraft.

Time may be displayed on a wrist watch which shows hours, minutes and seconds. Part-NCO states that an *"accurate time piece"* does not need to be an 'approved' type.

The required instruments can also be provided in the form of an integrated electronic display, commonly known as an Electronic Flight Information System (EFIS), and more informally as 'glass cockpit'. Any such integrated display has to be approved if installed in an aircraft with a C of A.

The guidance material for Part-NCO recommends that an aircraft operated under VFR should also be fitted with a 'slip' indicator.

If an aeroplane is to be operated by more than one crew member, it must be equipped with a form of 'intercom' system and a headset for each crew member.

If the aircraft has an electrical system which incorporates fuses, spare fuses must be carried.

Aeroplanes must have a **seat or berth** for each person on board aged 24 months or over. Each passenger seat must have **seat belt,** or restraining belts for each berth. Each flight crew seat must have a seat belt with an 'upper torso restraint system' (eg a diagonal shoulder strap or two shoulder straps), which has a single point release.

A Child Restraint Device (CRD) is required for each person on board younger than 24 months. If a CRD is used, there is an Alternative Means of Compliance (AMC) in PART-NCO which has detailed recommendations on the type, location and installation of a CRD.

Where required for the airspace being flown in, aeroplanes must be equipped with **radio communication equipment** capable of conducting two-way communication with the aeronautical stations and frequencies required to meet the airspace requirements. If radio communication equipment is required, it must have the capability to communicate on the aeronautical emergency frequency of 121.500MHz.

If an aeroplane is flying a route where navigation by reference to visual landmarks is not possible, it must be equipped with any navigation equipment required to navigate in accordance with the ATS flight plan (if applicable), or the applicable airspace requirements.

If required for the airspace being flown in, aeroplanes must be equipped with a **secondary surveillance radar (SSR) transponder** with all the required capabilities. For example some airspace may require that Mode C (altitude reporting) or Mode S capability transponders are carried.

Figure OP2.36
A communications radio and transponder installation in a Tecnam 2008.

## Safety equipment

There are several items of safety equipment which an aircraft may be required to carry, and many others which are advisable in certain situations.

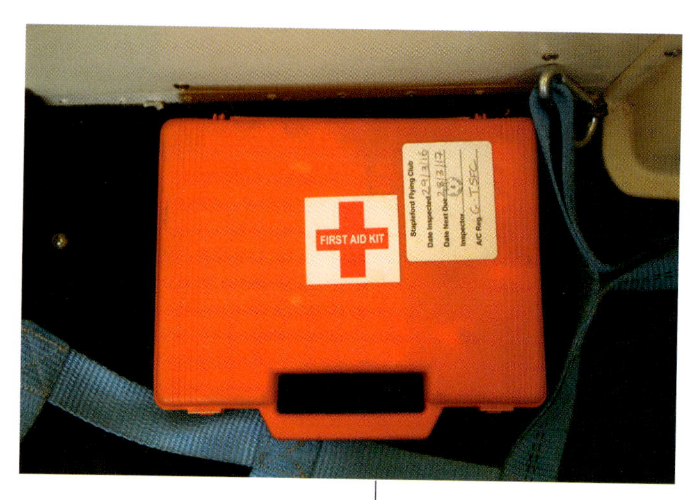


Figure OP2.37
An aircraft First Aid Kit, with inspection dates.

Aeroplanes must be equipped with a **first-aid kit** which is readily accessible for use and kept up-to-date (as certain medicines and contents have a limited 'shelf life'). For operations under Part-NCO, the first aid kit does not need to be an 'approved' type.

Aeroplanes must also be equipped with at least one hand **fire extinguisher** in the cockpit. This requirement does not apply to 'ELA1' aeroplanes. An ELA1 aircraft means an aeroplane with a Maximum Take-off Mass (MTOM) of 1,200kg or less that is not classified as a complex motor-powered aircraft; or a sailplane or powered sailplane of 1,200kg MTOM or less. Before flight, the fire extinguisher should be checked as being in place and properly secured. The latter is particularly important as during flight in turbulence or in the middle of an aerobatic manoeuvre, it can be very distracting to have a loose fire extinguisher flying around the cockpit! The extinguisher will probably have a gauge on the handle, whose needle should be in the green arc to show that the extinguisher is properly charged and pressurised. The extinguisher is likely to have a label showing the most recent inspection. If the last inspection is more than 12 months ago, it is worth asking questions of the maintenance organisation as most extinguisher manufacturers recommend inspection at least every 12 months.

Figure OP2.38
A typical cockpit fire extinguisher

Although not usually a mandatory item of safety equipment, many light aircraft are fitted with some type of 'Carbon Monoxide' detector. The method used for providing heated air in most light aircraft involves the possibility of **Carbon Monoxide** (**CO**) poisoning. Carbon monoxide is a colourless, odourless gas formed by incomplete combustion. It is virtually always present in exhaust gases, and it follows that a crack in an exhaust pipe leading through the cabin heater system could allow CO gas into the cockpit via the heated air. Carbon monoxide is a deadly poison, inhaling it leads to dizziness, headaches and blurred vision, a rapid impairment of normal mental functions and ultimately unconsciousness and death. Because CO poisoning affects the higher brain functions first, the victim may be completely unaware of any impairment, instead gradually falling into a dream-like 'dumb and happy' state. Many General Aviation aircraft are fitted with a CO detector somewhere on the instrument panel – usually in the form of a small plastic placard with a spot which will turn dark in the presence of carbon monoxide. These 'spot' CO detectors normally have a useful life of between three to six months (this 'life' should be stated on the detector) after which they should be replaced with a fresh unit.

Figure OP2.39
A 'badge-type' CO detector as commonly used in GA aircraft, if the spot turns dark, dangerous levels of CO are present. These type of CO detectors normally have a specified service life which may be a short as a few months.

Figure OP2.40
Typical light aircraft heating controls

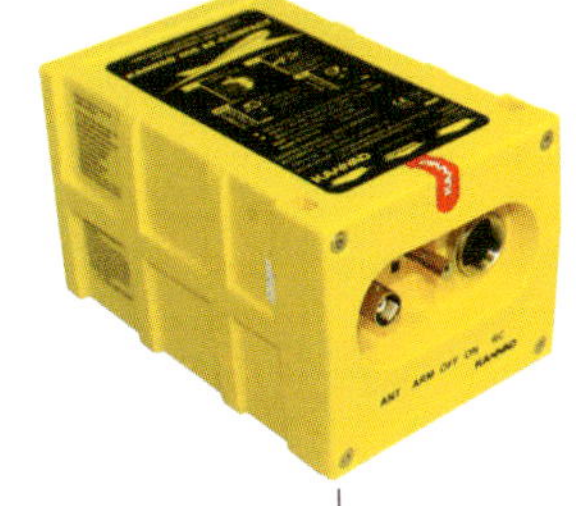

Figure OP2.41
An aviation ELT.

Part-NCO requires that aeroplanes are fitted with an **Emergency Locator Transmitter** (**ELT**). An ELT transmits signals on specified emergency frequencies (typically 121.500MHz and 406MHz) so that Search and Rescue (SAR) services can locate the ELT. If an aircraft was first issued with a Certificate of Airworthiness after 1st July 2008, the ELT must be an 'automatic' type – which will automatically activate in the event of high 'g' forces in an accident or possibly in the event of immersion in water.

If an aeroplane is certified for a maximum passenger seating of six or less, it is permissible for a passenger or crew member to carry a portable ELT or **Personal Locator Beacon** (**PLB**) in place of a fixed ELT. A PLB should also transmit on 121.500MHz and 406MHz and most modern PLBs can also transmit their GPS-derived position and a unique identifier. This allows the PLB's precise position anywhere in the world, and its unique identification, to be received by Search and Rescue services in as little as 5 minutes after activation. If the ELT or PLB is battery operated, the expiry date of the battery should be marked on the outside of the device. If a PLB is to be carried by a passenger, the Pilot-In-Command should brief that passenger on its characteristics and use before flight.

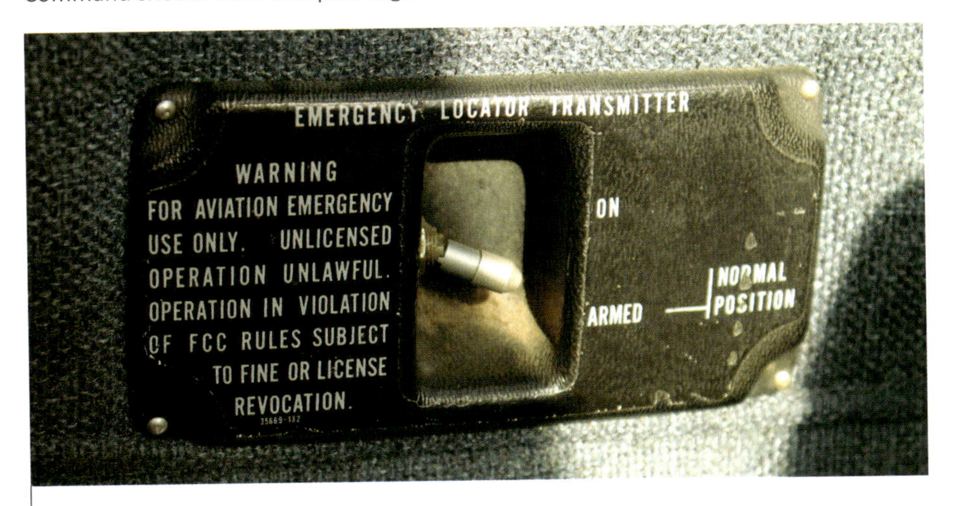


Figure OP2.42
The cockpit controls for an ELT may not be obvious, and often consist of a simple 'armed' or 'on' switch.

Figure OP2.43
A typical Personal Locator Beacon – PLB.

Part-NCO also requires that if a single-engine landplane is to be flown over water and beyond gliding distance of land, it must be equipped with a **lifejacket** (with a light) for every person on board, or an equivalent individual floatation device for each person younger than 24 months. Each lifejacket (or floatation device) must be worn or stowed in a position that is readily accessible from the seat or berth of the person for whose use it is provided. This requirement also applies when a single engine landplane is taking off or landing at a site where – in the opinion of the PIC – the take-off or approach path involves the risk of ditching in water.

When flying a single engine aircraft over water, it is strongly recommended that lifejackets are worn by all occupants. In the event of a ditching, lifejackets should not be inflated until the wearer is outside the aircraft.

Figure OP2.44
A typical 'constant wear' lifejacket.

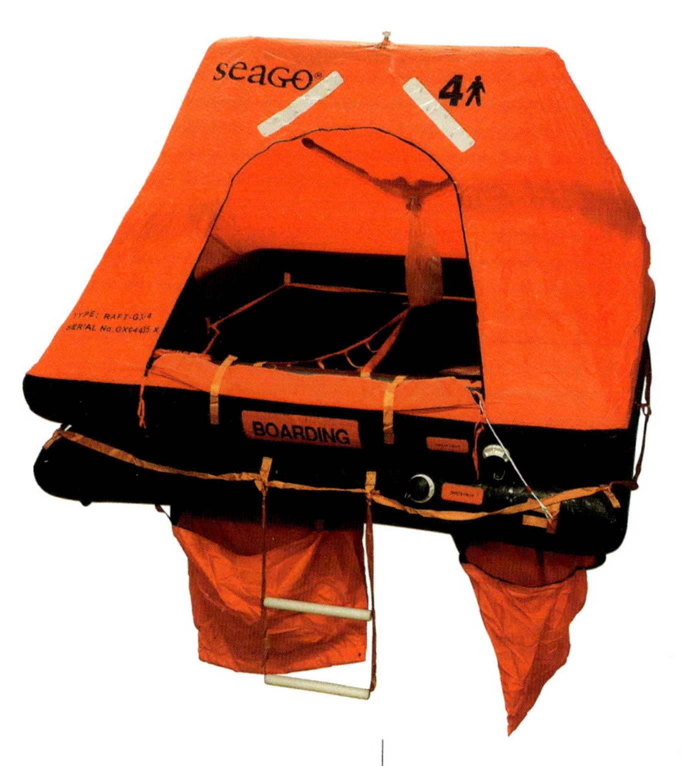


Figure OP2.45
A liferaft will increase survival times at sea to days and weeks rather than hours and minutes.

If any aeroplane (no matter how many engines it has) is operating at a distance from land where an emergency landing would be further away than 30 minutes at normal cruising speed – or 50 nautical miles, whichever is less – it must carry lifejackets for all occupants (or floatation devices for passengers under 24 months). Additionally, the PIC must consider the carriage of additional survival equipment to be used in the event of a ditching, including equipment for making distress signals; life-rafts capable of carrying all occupants, stowed ready to be used in an emergency; and other life-saving equipment as appropriate.

If an aeroplane is to be operated over areas in which search and rescue (SAR) operations could be especially difficult – such as particularly remote and inhospitable regions – it must be equipped with signalling devices and life-saving equipment, including means of sustaining life, appropriate to the area to be overflown.

Except when an aircraft is taking-off and landing at the same aerodrome or landing site, the operator must retain a list of the emergency and survival equipment carried on board the aircraft, ready for immediate communication to search and rescue services.

Figure OP2.46
A typical portable aviation oxygen system.

For practical purposes, in a 'non-pressurised' aeroplane the pressure altitude in the cabin, often called the 'cabin altitude', is approximately equivalent to the aircraft's altitude as indicated on the altimeter. The Pilot-In-Command must ensure that all flight crew members engaged in performing essential duties in flight use supplemental oxygen continuously whenever the PIC determines that at the altitude of the intended flight, lack of oxygen might impair the faculties of crew members. Additionally, the PIC must ensure that supplemental oxygen is available to passengers when lack of oxygen might harmfully affect those passengers.

If the Pilot-In-Command cannot determine how the lack of oxygen might affect the occupants on board, there is a stipulation that if a non-pressurised aeroplane is to be flown high enough that the pressure altitude in the cabin is between 10,000ft and 13,000ft, it must carry oxygen equipment with enough oxygen to supply all crew members for any period exceeding 30 minutes at that level. If the pressure altitude in the cabin will exceed 13,000ft, there must be enough oxygen to supply all crew and passengers for all the time that the pressure altitude in the cabin will be above 13,000ft.

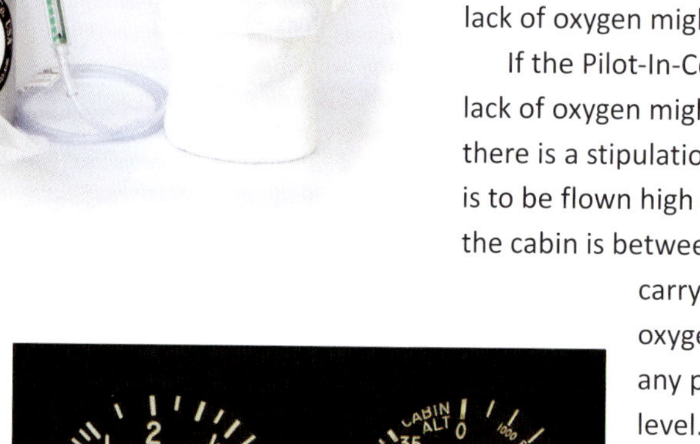


Figure OP2.47
Typical cabin pressure indicators in a General Aviation aircraft.

Intentionally Left Blank

## Progress check

9. What set of regulations govern the non-commercial operation of 'other than complex' aircraft?
10. What is a Certificate of Airworthiness (C of A)?
11. Who is ultimately responsible for the safety of the aircraft and of all crew members, passengers and cargo on board?
12. Who is responsible for recording all known or suspected defects of the aircraft in the aircraft technical log or journey log for the aircraft?
13. What is the Pilot-In-Command's responsibility in respect of checking weather before any flight?
14. What is an Aircraft Flight Manual (AFM)?
15. What is a Minimum Equipment List (MEL)?
16. What items of aircraft documentation must always be carried on board an aircraft as original documents, not copies?
17. Give some examples of 'dangerous goods' in relation to aircraft.
18. Under 'Part-NCO', what are the minimum fuel reserves for a VFR flight?
19. What are the Pilot-In-Command's responsibilities in regard to monitoring fuel reserves in flight?
20. What is the key 'source document' for checking the fuel and oil grades permitted in an aircraft?
21. Are 'AVGAS' and 'Jet A-1' fuels normally interchangeable in the same aircraft engine?
22. Is it permissible to have passengers on-board an aircraft when refuelling with AVGAS?
23. What is the absolute minimum aircraft instrumentation required for daytime VFR flight?
24. Other than in an 'ELA1' aeroplane, what specific types of portable safety/emergency equipment are mandatory in an aeroplane for all flights?
25. What are the 'Part-NCO' regulations in relation to ELTS and PLBs?

These questions are intended to test knowledge and reinforce some of the key learning points from this section. In answering these questions, a 'pass rate' of around 80% should be the target.

Model answers are found at pages 98-100.

# OP3 Avoidance of Hazards

Avoiding hazardous situations

Avoidance of wake turbulence

Progress check

# Avoidance of Hazards

## Avoiding hazardous situations

In terms of flight safety, a **hazard** can be considered as a situation, condition or an object which could endanger an aircraft or its occupants, reduce capability, or make the operation of the aircraft significantly more complex. In reality every flight must face some hazards (otherwise the aircraft would never start-up, let alone move), but a competent pilot will assess those hazards as a matter of course and take positive action to avoid the most severe dangers.

A common tool in aviation safety systems is a 'matrix' to assess the level of danger posed by specific situations. A very simple matrix to assess the level of danger posed by different hazards could look something like this:

| Hazard Class | Severity | | | | |
|---|---|---|---|---|---|
| | 1 | 2 | 3 | 4 | 5 |
| Potential effect on aircraft: | Aircraft destroyed or written off | Major damage or unserviceability. Major reduction in safety margin | Minor damage or unserviceability. Significant reduction in safety margin | Sight reduction in safety margin, minor reduction in aircraft capability | No effect on capability or safety margin |
| Potential effect on occupants: | Serious or fatal injuries | Serious injury | Minor injury | Discomfort or increase in workload | Inconvenience |

Figure OP3.1
A sample aviation safety matrix.

With a little thought it should be possible to assess potentially hazardous situations and prioritise actions to avoid the most severe hazards.

To avoid a hazardous situation, the pilot first has to recognise it. The ability to recognise potentially hazardous situations, preferably long before they can have any direct effect on the safety of a flight, is traditionally held to be one of the benefits of experience. This viewpoint can be summed-up in the maxim:

*"Experience is the ability to recognise a mistake before you make it again"*.

The problem with an experience-based approach to recognising hazards is that, almost by definition, the pilot can only gain experience by making mistakes. If follows that, at times, only luck will dictate how serious the consequences of those mistakes will be.

A more enlightened approach is to use the experiences of other pilots as a way of learning more about hazardous situations, without actually having to experience them first-hand. In business-speak, this could be said to be leveraging the experiences of others. Aviation legislation requires not only that accidents are reported and investigated, but that incidents and potentially unsafe situations are also reported. Many states also have confidential reporting systems where pilots, engineers, controllers and others engaged in aviation can confess their own mistakes or raise safety concerns, without publically identifying themselves. For many pilots such accident, incident and safety reports are essential reading. Whilst this might appear to be morbid curiosity of the same kind that makes drivers slow down to view the aftermath of a road accident, in fact the educational value of reading such reports is a widely recognised. By reading accident, incident and safety reports, most pilots will recognise situations that they have faced or can relate to, and very often the safety lessons are evident.

Reading safety reports regularly will also reinforce the fact that the causes of the majority of accidents and serious incidents are regular and reoccurring themes (those working in aviation safety are prone to saying, "*There are no new accidents*"). Analysis of General Aviation accident reports, even across different states and different periods, tends to identify the same key causes of serious accidents. One such analysis by the UK Civil Aviation Authority is typical, it identified six recurring causes of serious accidents and incidents to General Aviation aircraft:

- Loss of Control
- Controlled Flight into Terrain (CFIT)
- Airborne Conflict
- Runway Excursion
- Airspace Infringement
- Human Factors in the GA Cockpit

Each of these common accident causes tend to arise out of certain hazardous situations, which are summarised below:

**Loss of Control**

In VFR flight, this type of accident often involves a stall/spin at low level. This may occur during extreme pitch and roll attitudes at low level (for example aerobatic manoeuvres) and/or as a result of pilot distraction. Loss of control may also occur on take-off or landing due to incorrect piloting technique or poor skills. A less serious loss of control issue is a mishandled landing or landing and/or bouncing repeatedly on the nosewheel.

This hazardous situation can be avoided by always making the flying of the aeroplane the number one priority, maintaining handling skills and paying close attention to the airspeed (or angle of attack, if indicated) in relation to the manoeuvre being flown. Aerobatics and other manoeuvres involving large pitch and roll angles should always be practiced at a safe height. Landing accidents are almost always avoidable, if the pilot had elected to go-around at the initial signs of trouble.

Figure OP3.2

Loss of Control (LOC), especially on landing, is a common cause of aircraft accidents – such as this collapsed nose wheel.

Figure OP3.3
Controlled Flight into Terrain (CFIT) occurs where an aeroplane flies into the ground due to a failure to maintain a safe height. This may occur when a pilot attempting to fly VFR, enters IMC conditions – such as low cloud or fog.

### Controlled Flight into Terrain (CFIT)

This term describes the situation where an aeroplane flies into the ground due to a failure to maintain a safe height. In the VFR context, CFIT is most likely to occur when Visual Meteorological Conditions (VMC) flight is attempted in Instrument Meteorological Conditions (IMC) weather – for example attempting to fly visually in cloud and/or poor visibility. This type of hazardous situation is sometimes described as 'VFR into IMC', in other words the flight was intended to be a VFR operation, but ended up in IMC.

Avoidance of this hazardous situation is best achieved by maintaining at least VMC minima when flying VFR (as the pilot is legally required to do) and in particular avoiding the potentially lethal situation of attempted VFR flight into an area of low cloud, poor visibility and high ground. In most CFIT accidents the pilot did not know his/her true position, or had lost situational awareness in some other way.

### Airborne Conflict

Getting too close to other aircraft unintentionally can lead to an 'airprox' (a situation in which the distance between aircraft as well as their relative positions and speed mean that the safety of the aircraft may have been compromised), or even a collision. Airborne conflict in VMC flight normally occurs because at least one of the pilots did not see the other aircraft with enough time to maintain a safe separation. As a general rule, airborne conflict in VMC is more likely to occur in uncontrolled airspace or near uncontrolled airfields, especially in the airfield circuit.

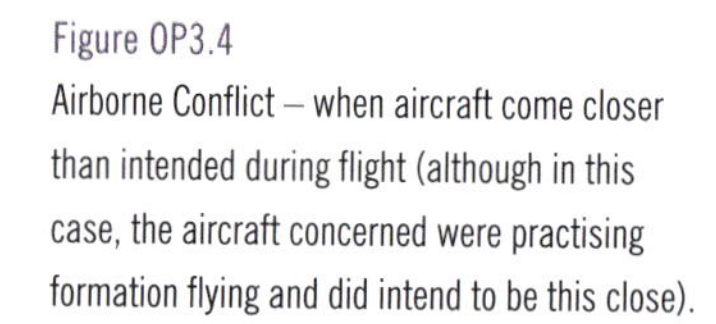

Figure OP3.4
Airborne Conflict – when aircraft come closer than intended during flight (although in this case, the aircraft concerned were practising formation flying and did intend to be this close).

The risk of airborne conflict can be minimised by always maintaining a good visual lookout at all stages of flight. Additionally, following correct procedures (for example when joining and flying in the airfield circuit) will help avoid airborne conflict.

### Runway Excursion

This is the situation where an aircraft leaves the runway in an unintended manner, normally by running off the end or side of the runway. This can occur on either take-off or landing and is more likely to occur when the runway distance is close to (or less than) that required for the aircraft to take-off or land in the prevailing conditions – eg surface wind, temperature, aircraft weight etc. Poor piloting skill, and in particular failure to use the correct take-off or landing technique (such as the correct approach speed), is a common factor in runway excursions involving GA aircraft. Runway 'contamination' (for example a wet runway) will increase the aircraft's take-off and landing distance and so increase the risk of runway excursion.

Any time the aircraft will be operating on a runway with dimensions close to the take-off or landing distance required, particular care must be taken in calculating take-off and landing performance, knowing the correct technique (in particular airspeed and aircraft configuration) and applying that technique. This hazardous situation can also be avoided in flight by making an early decision to abandon a take-off, or go-around from an approach to land, if the risk of a runway excursion becomes apparent.

Figure OP3.5
Runway Excursion – leaving the runway in an unplanned way. Can be the result of several factors, including attempting to use a runway that is too short for the aircraft, pilot handling errors and incorrect take-off/landing technique.

### Airspace Infringement

This situation normally arises when an aircraft enters controlled or notified airspace without first obtaining the necessary clearance or establishing communications. VMC airspace infringements mostly occur because the pilot does not know the aircraft's actual position in relation to notified airspace, or even because the pilot is unaware of the existence of the notified airspace. Inadequate pre-flight planning and poor in-flight navigation are common factors in airspace infringements.

Airspace infringement can be avoided through proper pre-flight planning and careful in-flight navigation, maintaining an accurate assessment of the aircraft's lateral and vertical position in relation to controlled airspace. Contacting the appropriate ATS unit and requesting clearance to cross controlled or notified airspace, where appropriate, is most often simpler and safer than attempting to navigate around the edge of airspace boundaries.

Figure OP3.6
Airspace Infringement – careful pre-flight planning, accurate in-flight navigation and the use of moving map GPS devices go a long way to avoiding airspace infringement.

Figure OP3.7
As you might expect, 'human factors' incidents are more likely to occur when a single pilot is in control of a flight, rather than in two-crew operations.

**Human Factors in the GA Cockpit**

A typical General Aviation (GA) flight is a single-crew operation conducted in a relatively informal atmosphere. This means that many of the checks and safeguards of a commercial operation – for example two-crew flight deck, strict Standard Operating Procedures (SOP), controlled environment, management oversight etc. are not applicable. In this aspect the average GA flight is much more susceptible to the performance of a single person – namely the pilot – than most commercial operations.

The requirement for a single pilot to recognise and avoid threats and operating errors is one of the prime reasons that the pilot of even the smallest and most simple aircraft must be competent in Threat and Error Management (TEM) techniques. It is also important that a pilot remains alert to his or her own state of mind, traits and weaknesses. Different personality traits will cause some pilots to be more likely to get into certain hazardous situations. The acceptance of this fact is an important factor in avoiding dangerous circumstances and maintaining a good margin of safety.

It is worth emphasising that the hazardous situations described above are evidently not the only ones which a pilot can encounter, merely those which are most often implicated in serious accidents and incidents involving GA aircraft. For example, flight into icing conditions in a non de-iced aircraft is also a hazardous situation, but the fact that fewer accidents happen this way is probably an indication that this is a rarer event. In the same way, flight into or close to an active thunderstorm is very obviously a hazardous situation, the dangers of which are well-understood and widely-publicised, so it is not surprising that relatively few accidents occur in this way. It cannot be over-emphasised that very often aviation safety is a matter of common sense. If something looks wrong, or even just 'feels' wrong or risky, there is a very good chance that a hazardous situation is developing.

Certain actions or behaviours by a pilot can increase the risk of a hazardous situation developing, or make the potential consequences of a hazardous situation more serious. These include:

- Rule-breaking;
- Failing to follow established operating procedures or 'best practice';
- Operating an aircraft close to, or beyond, its limitations (including performance limits);
- Unfamiliar situations or circumstances;
- Insufficient pre-flight preparation.

## Avoidance of wake turbulence

Wake turbulence is a term to describe the specific turbulence which occurs behind the wing of an aircraft (or rotor disc of a helicopter) passing through the air. Wake turbulence can be serious enough that in the worst case scenario – for example a small, light aircraft following a large, heavy aircraft – the following aircraft may experience loss of control.

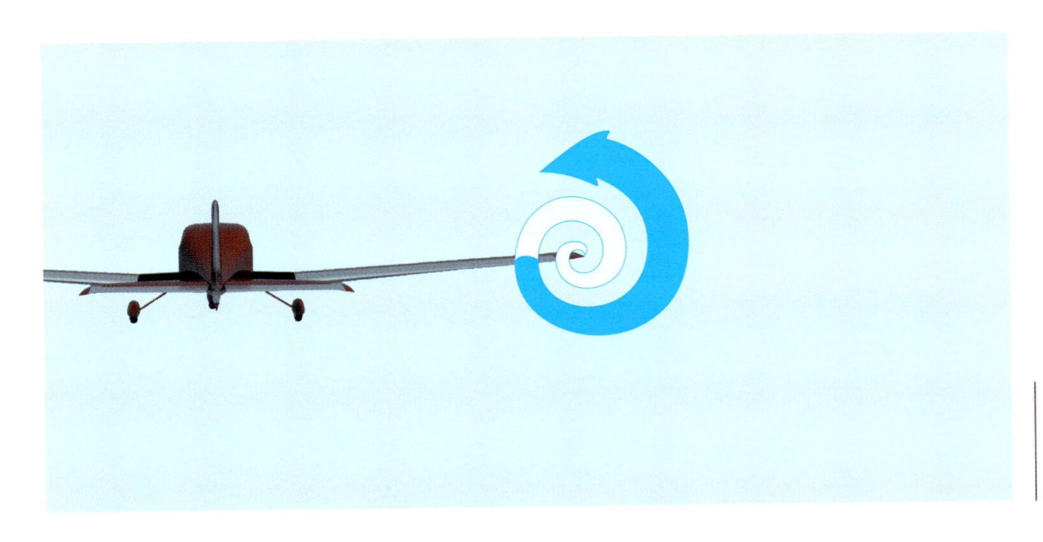

Figure OP3.8
Any wing (or rotor blade) moving through the air will generate wake turbulence, most especially at the wing tips.

Wake turbulence will occur any time a wing (or rotor blade) is generating lift. A wing generates lift by creating a pressure differential above and below the wing, with higher pressure below the wing and lower pressure above it. Air tends to move from high pressure to low pressure and so higher pressure air under the wing tends to move outwards (and lower pressure above the wing tends to move inwards). At the wingtip the air 'curls over' from under the wing to above it, and in that process a fast-rotating vortex of air is formed. When generated by a large, heavy aircraft, the vortices generated from the wing tips can be up to 30 metres across and at their core – perhaps one metre across – the rotating air can reach a velocity of up to 100 metres per second (around 200 miles per hour). Any aircraft encountering such a vortex will experience significant disturbance, the smaller and lighter the aircraft (and the shorter its wingspan), the more it will be disturbed and the greater the risk of loss of control.

Figure OP3.9
Even the smallest aircraft wings generate wake vortices and wake turbulence.

There are other elements to wake turbulence, such as small-scale vortices shed along the wing trailing edge, and a general 'downwash' of descending air behind the wing, but it is the wingtip vortices that present the greatest danger to other aircraft.

Once wingtip vortices have left the wing, they begin to descend at approximately 300-500 feet per minute, until levelling out approximately 1000ft lower than when they were created. If the vortices reach the surface, they then tend to move outwards at a speed of about 3 knots (in still air conditions). The ideal atmospheric conditions for wake vortices to persist are zero or very light wind speed in smooth and stable air and the vortices can persist for approximately 3 minutes, occasionally longer. Vortices are generally considered to begin when an aeroplane 'rotates' on take-off and to continue until touchdown on landing. The strength of wing tip vortices generated by an aeroplane increase with aircraft weight and also increase as the aircraft flies more slowly. So, operating behind a large heavy aircraft, flying slowly, is a prime area to encounter wake turbulence.

Figure OP3.9a
Sometimes wake turbulence can be seen when an aircraft flies through cloud or fog, such as here behind an Embraer ERJ-195…

Figure OP3.9b
… and an Airbus A319.

Figure OP3.10
If taking-off behind a larger aircraft, aim to avoid that aircraft's flight path.

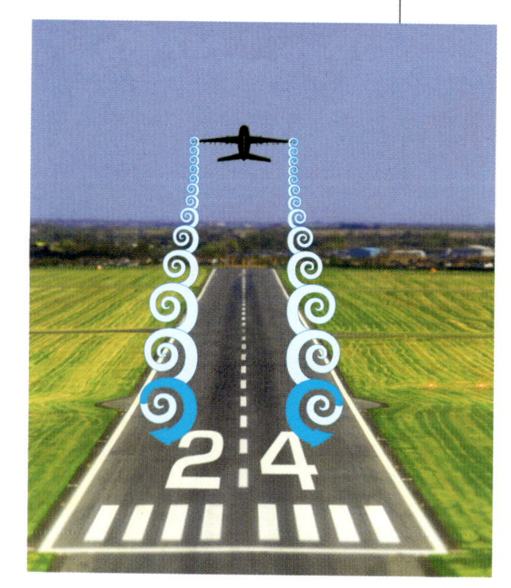


In most atmospheric conditions, wake turbulence is invisible and all but impossible to detect (although a ground observer will occasionally hear wake vortices after an aircraft has passed low overhead, or see the effect on clouds or fog, trees or even roof tiles). It follows that the only effective method to prevent an encounter with wake turbulence is to avoid the region behind and below a larger aircraft, or if that is not practicable, allow sufficient separation for the wake vortices to decay.

In the take-off phase, the pilot of an aircraft following a larger aircraft should specifically note the larger aircraft's rotation point and climb-out path. The pilot of the following aircraft should then aim, if possible, to get airborne before that point and avoid flying below or downwind of the leading aircraft's climb-out path (because the vortices will descend and drift downwind). On the longer runways from which large aircraft operate, it should not be difficult – when at a safe height – to turn slightly to stay upwind of a leading aircraft's climb path. It is worth remembering that airliners tend to have fairly spectacular rates of climb just after take-off and it's highly unlikely that an average light aircraft will be able to out-climb an airliner. Therefore staying above the leading aircraft's climb-out path is not likely to be feasible. Even when taking-off from a different runway to the leading aircraft, wake turbulence could still affect a following aircraft departing from a crossing runway, or a parallel runway.

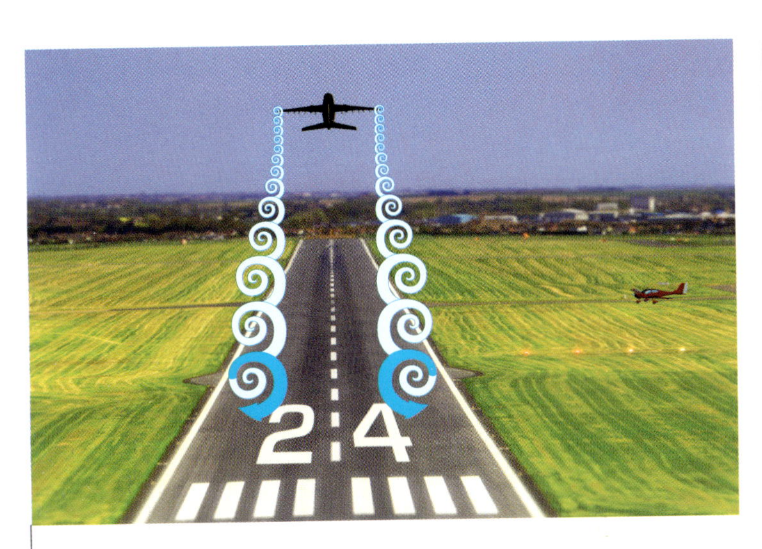


Figure OP3.12
Even when taking-off from different runways, wake turbulence may be an issue.

Figure OP3.13
You do not have to be directly following an aircraft to be affected by its wake turbulence.

In cruising flight wake turbulence incidents are less common, probably because small and large aircraft generally stay well apart and standard ATC separation rules reduce the risk of encountering wing tip vortices. However, studies have found that a large heavy aircraft generates the strongest wake turbulence when flying slowly in a gear-up and flaps-up condition (often referred to as a 'clean' configuration).

The greatest number of serious wake turbulence encounters occur in the approach and landing phase. Again the golden rule when following a larger aircraft is to avoid getting below or downwind of its flight path (indeed an American study of wake-turbulence incidents and accidents showed that in all but one case, the following aircraft was below the leading aircraft's flight path). Airliners tend to fly relatively shallow instrument approaches with a 'glide path' (approach) angle of about 3°, which is a good deal shallower than the angle at which light aircraft tend to approach. A 3° glide path equates to a height change of around 300ft per nautical mile, thus an aircraft following a 3° glide path will be at around 300ft above the runway when one mile from the runway, 600ft at two miles, 900ft at three miles etc. Approaching above this glide path angle and aiming to touchdown beyond the leading aircraft's landing point should avoid the most risky area for wake turbulence. However, at times airliners can follow a surprisingly steep glideslope – especially if flying a visual approach – and wake turbulence can be expected to be at its strongest just as the aircraft touches down. The pilot of a smaller following aircraft should judge the leading aircraft's approach path and manoeuvre to stay above and upwind

Figure OP3.11
Careful observation of the leading aircraft's climb-out path is key to avoiding its wake turbulence.

Figure OP3.14
Large aircraft on approach to land tend to generate to strongest wake turbulence in the area behind and below their flightpath.

Figure OP3.15
Careful observation of the leading aircraft's approach and landing path is key to avoiding its wake turbulence.

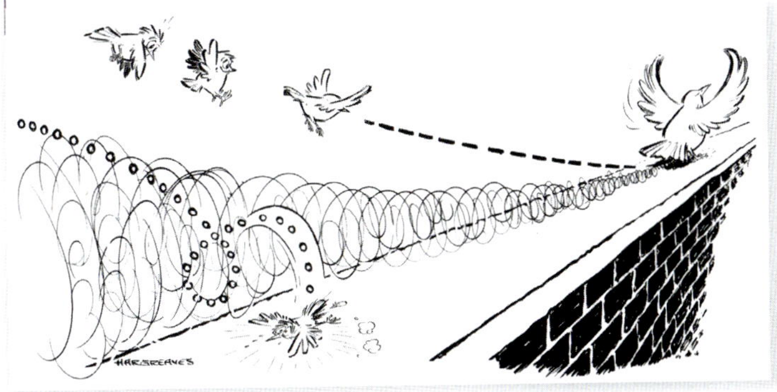

Figure OP3.17
Wake turbulence behind a Boeing 737 on approach, made visible as it passes through a cloud.

Figure OP3.16
The 'golden rule' of wake turbulence is to avoid the areas where is might exist.

of it and aim to land beyond the leading aircraft's touchdown point; assuming sufficient runway is available. As with take-off, wake turbulence may affect a following aircraft even if landing on a different runway from that of the leading aircraft. Crossing the leading aircraft's approach path, or a light wind drifting vortices into the following aircraft's flight path, can easily lead to an encounter with wake turbulence.

Wake turbulence may also be a hazard to a following aircraft landing behind a departing aircraft. When landing on the same runway as a larger departing aircraft, or a crossing runway, the aim should be to touch down before the leading aircraft's rotation point and be aware of the possible drift of vortices if using a parallel or adjacent runway.

In order to establish minimum separation for wake turbulence avoidance, Eurocontrol (an organisation which co-ordinates European air traffic services) have established seven wake turbulence categories, based on an aircraft's maximum certified take-off weight and wingspan. Those wake turbulence categories are:

Figure OP3.18
The European wake turbulence categories.

| | Category | Maximum certified take-off mass /wing span | Examples of aircraft in category |
|---|---|---|---|
| **Super Heavy** | 'Cat-A' | More than 100,000kg / 72m-80m | A380, An-124 |
| **Upper Heavy** | 'Cat-B' | More than 100,000kg / 60m-72m | A330, A340, B747, B777, B787 |
| **Lower Heavy** | 'Cat-C' | More than 100,000kg / less than 60m | B757, B767, MD11 |
| **Upper Medium** | 'Cat-D' | Less than 100,000kg / more than 32m | A320 series (A318-A321), B737 series, |
| **Lower Medium** | 'Cat-E' | Less than 100,000kg / less than 32m | ATR72, CRJ, Q-400, Embraer E135 to E195 |
| **Light** | 'Cat-F' | Less than 15,000kg | Beech turboprops, SF340, LearJets, Cessna Citations, C150, PA28 |

Figure OP3.19
An example of a 'super heavy' aircraft – the Airbus A380.

Figure OP3.20
An example of an 'upper heavy' category aircraft – a Boeing 777.

Figure OP3.21
An example of a 'lower heavy' category aircraft – a Boeing 757.

Figure OP3.22
An example of an 'upper medium' category aircraft – an Airbus A320.

Figure OP3.23
An example of a 'lower medium' category aircraft – a 'Dash 8' Q400.

Figure OP3.24
An example of a 'light' category aircraft – a Beechcraft Kingair.

Sometimes aircraft can be moved into a different category based on analysis of its characteristics. It is not necessary to memorise these criteria, however Eurocontrol have set-out minimum separation distances based on these categories. In the following tables, it is assumed that the following aircraft is in the 'Light' category.

**Minimum distance separation, approach and departure:**

| Leading aircraft category | Minimum distance to following 'Light' category aircraft in Nautical Miles (nm) |
|---|---|
| Super Heavy | 8nm |
| Upper Heavy | 7nm |
| Lower Heavy | 6nm |
| Upper Medium | 5nm |
| Lower Medium | 4nm |
| Light | 3nm |

Figure OP3.25
Avoiding wake turbulence – recommended minimum distance separation, approach and departure.

**Minimum time separation, departure:**

| Leading aircraft category | Minimum time to following 'Light' category aircraft in minutes/seconds |
|---|---|
| Super Heavy | 3 minutes |
| Upper Heavy | 140 seconds |
| Lower Heavy | 2 minutes |
| Upper Medium | 2 minutes |
| Lower Medium | 100 seconds |
| Light | 80 seconds |

Figure OP3.26
Avoiding wake turbulence – recommended minimum time separation on departure.

At almost any airport where 'Light' category aircraft mix with aircraft in other categories (mostly airliners), some form of ATC will be in operation. The exact application of the above criteria are at the discretion of ATC, as a general rule the pilot of the following aircraft will normally be cautioned of the risk of 'Wake Turbulence' and the appropriate separation minima may be stated. On take-off, ATC will not normally issue a clearance to take-off until the appropriate time minima has passed. In all cases, the final responsibility for avoiding wake turbulence rests with the pilot of the following aircraft, who can exercise his or her discretion to use an increased distance or time separation whenever it seems necessary to do so.

It is worth noting that some form of wake turbulence exists behind all aeroplanes – most pilots who have practiced formation flying will have had the experience of encountering vortices when flying close behind even a small aircraft. Very occasionally, wake turbulence accidents have occurred where both the leading aircraft and the following aircraft were in the 'light' category, usually in atmospheric conditions (eg calm or very light cross-winds) that were ideal for wing tip vortices to persist.

Figure OP3.27
Helicopters also generate wake turbulence, which can be considerably stronger than for a fixed-wing aircraft of the same size/weight.

Figure OP3.27
It is recommended that aircraft avoid a helicopter in flight or hover taxiing by at least three times the rotor disc diameter.

The above minima are based on 'fixed wing' aeroplanes, however helicopters also generate wake turbulence and the evidence is that a helicopter generates stronger wake turbulence than a fixed wing aeroplane of the same weight. Additionally, helicopter wake turbulence is less predictable than that for fixed wing aeroplanes and seems to cover a larger area than that generated by a fixed wing aeroplane of similar size and weight. Wake turbulence generated from helicopters seems to be at its strongest when the helicopter is flying relatively slowly – between 20 and 50 knots. When a helicopter is hovering or hover-taxiing, the rotor blade downwash and vortices expand outwards in all directions. It is recommended that light aircraft should avoid helicopters hovering or hover-taxiing by a distance equivalent to at least three times the diameter of rotor blades, and stay upwind of the helicopter if possible.

The avoidance of wake turbulence starts with a recognition of its dangers and can be summarised in a few key points:

- The larger, heavier and more slowly an aircraft is flying, the greater the wake turbulence it generates.
- Avoid flying in the area behind and below a larger aircraft.
- Adhere to the wake turbulence minima, increase distance/time separation if necessary.
- Be aware that helicopters generate significant wake turbulence, stronger than an aeroplane of the same size/weight

## Progress check

26. In terms of flight safety, how can a 'hazard' be defined?
27. How is wake turbulence generated and where does is exist?
28. What are the ideal atmospheric conditions for wake vortices to persist?
29. In which flight phases are wake turbulence encounters considered to be the most dangerous?
30. What is the Eurocontrol minimum separation distance for a light aircraft approaching to land behind an Airbus A320 or Boeing 737 ('Upper Medium' category or 'Cat-D')?
31. What is the Eurocontrol minimum time separation for a light aircraft departing behind an Airbus A320 or Boeing 737 ('Upper Medium' category or 'Cat-D')?
32. What are the characteristics of wake turbulence produced by a helicopter, as compared to wake turbulence produced by an aeroplane?
33. Up to what approximate distance is helicopter wake turbulence considered to be a hazard around a hovering or 'hover-taxiing' helicopter?

These questions are intended to test knowledge and reinforce some of the key learning points from this section. In answering these questions, a 'pass rate' of around 80% should be the target.

Model answers are found at page 100.

# OP4 Search and Rescue Procedures

Principles of search and rescue procedures

Search and rescue signals

Progress check

# OP4 Search and Rescue Procedures

## Principles of search and rescue procedures

Flying over some of the more densely populated parts of Europe, it can be difficult to believe that an aeroplane making a forced landing could go unnoticed for very long. Even if a forced landing is not seen by witnesses, with a radio in the aircraft and a mobile phone in the pocket, surely help can be on its way in any circumstances within moments?

Figure OP4.1
This inhospitable terrain – (the Scottish hills in winter) is less than 10 minutes flying time from a major airport (Inverness).

Figure OP4.2
The sea, and indeed any large stretch of open water, is also regarded as inhospitable terrain.

However, fly for just another 15 or 20 minutes and the situation can change completely. Even within Western Europe a light aircraft pilot could easily be flying over inhospitable high ground with sparse habitation and few roads; or approaching an extensive mountain range with peaks significantly higher than 10,000ft, or crossing the open sea well beyond gliding distance of land. Any of these situations should cause a pilot to give serious thought about how quickly, and how easily, help could arrive on scene in the event of an unplanned landing. Furthermore, for help to arrive someone, somewhere, needs to know that urgent assistance is required and also needs to have at least some idea of where to send that help. The more quickly that assistance is sent and the more accurately the rescue services know where to go, the better the prospects for those waiting for help to arrive.

ICAO recommend that a state should establish a **Search And Rescue** (**SAR**) organisation within its territory. In practice, each state normally provides some form of SAR service within approximately the area covered by its Flight Information Regions (FIR) and sometimes beyond – for example over an adjacent area of sea. Within each SAR region there should be a **Rescue Coordination Centre** (**RCC**), which is responsible for organising search and rescue services and for coordinating search and rescue operations within its area of coverage.

Figure OP4.3
A typical Rescue Coordination Centre.

Any time a flight is planned over areas which are difficult for SAR operations, extra consideration needs to be given to how the details of the flight will be notified to the authorities. Such inhospitable areas may include extensive areas of high ground and mountains, sparsely populated regions and the open sea or large lakes – a state's AIP may stipulate specific areas which are considered to be particularly difficult for SAR services. According to Part-NCO *"areas in which search and rescue would be especially difficult"* means:

- areas designated by the competent authority; or
- areas that are largely uninhabited.

One way of notifying flight details is to file a **full flight plan** for the flight. The full flight plan contains details of the flight including aircraft type, occupants, routing, emergency equipment carried etc. This information is passed to selected **Air Traffic Service Units** (**ATSU**) along the route and when the flight departs, the flight plan is 'activated' and an **Estimated Time of Arrival** (**ETA**) for the destination is established. When the flight arrives at its destination an 'arrival' message may be sent to confirm the safe arrival of the flight and the flight plan is 'closed'. If the flight does not arrive at the destination, action should be started to locate the aircraft, for example by contacting ATSUs along the aircraft's flight planned route. If the aircraft still cannot be located, the relevant RCC will be contacted and ultimately full SAR operations may be initiated. Even if a full flight plan is not filed, at the flight planning stage it may be prudent to plan to remain in radio contact with ATSUs along the route offering either Air Traffic Control (ATC) or Flight Information Service (FIS). In the event that the aircraft reports an emergency situation, or goes missing, the last ATSU in contact with the aircraft is normally responsible for initiating the appropriate action.

Figure OP4.4
By filing a full flight plan, the pilot formally notifies details of the flight to the Air Traffic Services, including any ATS units at the departure and destination airfields.

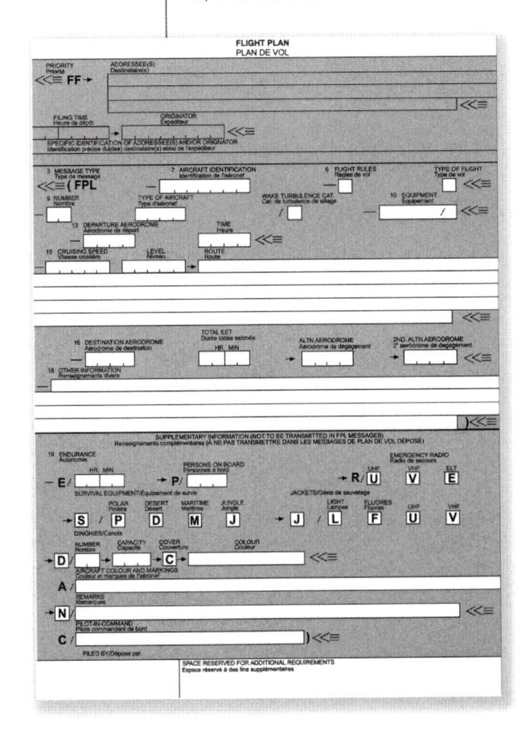

FLIGHT PLAN
PLAN DE VOL

PRIORITY / Priorité — FF
ADDRESSEE(S) / Destinataire(s)
FILING TIME / Heure de dépôt
ORIGINATOR / Expéditeur
SPECIFIC IDENTIFICATION OF ADDRESSEE(S) AND/OR ORIGINATOR / Identification précise du(des) destinataire(s) et/ou de l'expéditeur

3 MESSAGE TYPE / Type de message — ( FPL
7 AIRCRAFT IDENTIFICATION / Identification de l'aéronef
8 FLIGHT RULES / Règles de vol
TYPE OF FLIGHT / Type de vol
9 NUMBER / Nombre
TYPE OF AIRCRAFT / Type d'aéronef
WAKE TURBULENCE CAT. / Cat. de turbulence de sillage
10 EQUIPMENT / Équipement
13 DEPARTURE AERODROME / Aérodrome de départ
TIME / Heure
15 CRUISING SPEED / Vitesse croisière
LEVEL / Niveau
ROUTE / Route
16 DESTINATION AERODROME / Aérodrome de destination
TOTAL EET / Durée totale estimée — HR. MIN
ALTN AERODROME / Aérodrome de dégagement
2ND. ALTN AERODROME / 2e aérodrome de dégagement
18 OTHER INFORMATION / Renseignements divers

SUPPLEMENTARY INFORMATION (NOT TO BE TRANSMITTED IN FPL MESSAGES)
Renseignements complémentaires (À NE PAS TRANSMETTRE DANS LES MESSAGES DE PLAN DE VOL DÉPOSÉ)

19 ENDURANCE / Autonomie — HR. MIN — E/
PERSONS ON BOARD / Personnes à bord — P/
EMERGENCY RADIO / Radio de secours — R/ UHF U VHF V ELT E
SURVIVAL EQUIPMENT/Équipement de survie — S / POLAR Polaire P, DESERT Désert D, MARITIME Maritime M, JUNGLE Jungle J
JACKETS/Gilets de sauvetage — J / LIGHT Lampes L, FLUORES Fluores F, UHF U, VHF V
DINGHIES/Canots — D/ NUMBER Nombre, CAPACITY Capacité, COVER Couverture C, COLOUR Couleur
AIRCRAFT COLOUR AND MARKINGS / Couleur et marques de l'aéronef — A/
REMARKS / Remarques — N/
PILOT-IN-COMMAND / Pilote commandant de bord — C/
FILED BY/Déposé par
SPACE RESERVED FOR ADDITIONAL REQUIREMENTS
Espace réservé à des fins supplémentaires

Also at the pre-flight planning stage, the pilot should consider what equipment needs to be carried on board the aircraft. A state may specify certain items of emergency or survival equipment that are to be carried for flight over particular areas or regions. In accordance with Part-NCO, an aircraft should be fitted with an Emergency Locator Transmitter (ELT) or carry a Personal Locator Beacon (PLB) for all flights, and the pilot should be familiar with the operation of these items. An ELT is equipment that broadcasts distinctive signals on designated frequencies and may be activated by impact or manually activated. A PLB is an emergency beacon other than an ELT that broadcasts distinctive signals on designated frequencies, is standalone, portable and is manually activated by the survivors.

For flight over water and beyond gliding distance of land, lifejackets should be carried for all occupants. Part-NCO requires that the lifejackets must be "*...accessible from the seat or berth of the person for whose use it is provided, with a safety belt or a restraint system fastened*". In a single-engine aircraft the normal practice is that lifejackets should worn (but not inflated) by all occupants. Incidentally, seat cushions are not normally considered to be flotation devices.

According to Part-NCO, if an aeroplane is to be operated more than 50 nautical miles from land suitable for an emergency landing (or 30 minutes at normal cruising speed, whichever is the lesser), the Pilot-In-Command should make a risk assessment taking into account:

- sea state;
- sea and air temperatures;
- the distance from land suitable for making an emergency landing; and
- the availability of search and rescue facilities.

Figure OP4.5
An approximate guide to average survival times in a near-calm sea.

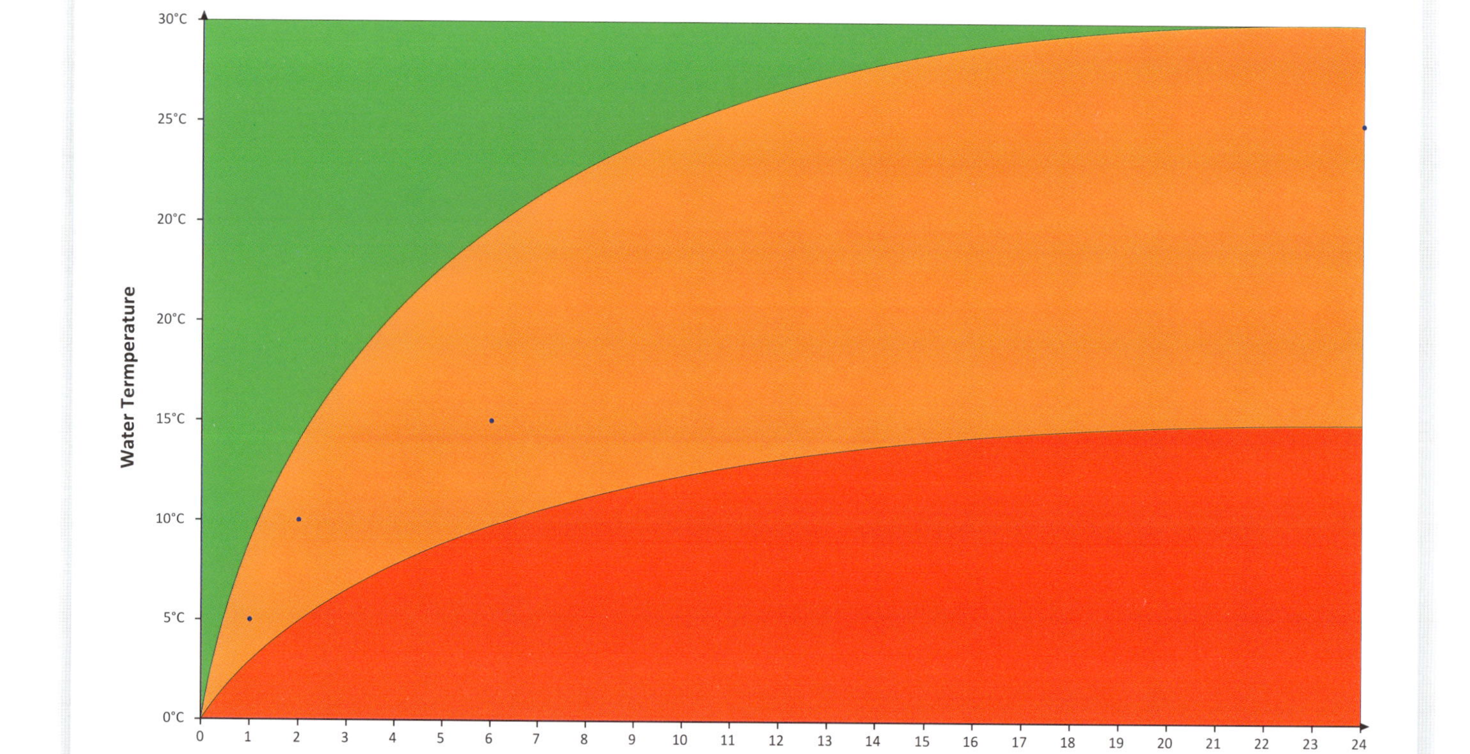

Based on that risk assessment, the PIC can decide whether to carry survival equipment such as:

- equipment for making the distress signals;
- liferafts to carry all persons on board, stowed for ready use in emergency; and
- life-saving equipment, to provide the means of sustaining life, as appropriate.

If an aircraft is to operate over a land area where SAR is especially difficult, Part-NCO recommends that the aircraft should carry:

- signalling equipment to make the distress signal;
- at least one survival ELT, or a PLB, carried by the Pilot-In-Command or a passenger; and
- additional survival equipment for the route to be flown, taking account of the number of persons on board.

In the case of a single-engine aircraft, if it will not be operating more than 30 minutes cruising time from an area not considered difficult for SAR, 'additional survival equipment' need not be carried.

On a practical note, when considering the land terrain to be overflown it is worth remembering the advice that military aircrew tend to quote – that the aircraft should carry the clothing that the pilot would want to wear for walking out of that area. For example, even in mid-summer the top of a mountain can be a surprisingly cold place, especially if the weather closes in. Simple precautions such as a warm jacket in the back of the aircraft, or a survival blanket packed in the pilot's flight bag, could make all the difference in such a situation.

| Wind | Temperature in Celsius (°C) | | | | | | | |
|---|---|---|---|---|---|---|---|---|
| (mph) | 10 | 5 | 0 | -5 | -10 | -15 | -20 | -25 |
| 10 | 5 | -1 | -7 | -13 | -19 | -25 | -31 | -37 |
| 20 | 0 | -6 | -13 | -20 | -27 | -34 | -41 | -48 |
| 30 | -1 | -9 | -16 | -24 | -31 | -39 | -46 | -54 |
| 40 | -2 | -10 | -18 | -26 | -34 | -41 | -49 | -57 |
| 50 | -3 | -11 | -19 | -27 | -35 | -43 | -50 | -58 |
| 60 | -3 | -11 | -19 | -27 | -35 | -43 | -50 | -58 |
| 70 | -3 | -10 | -18 | -26 | -34 | -42 | -50 | -57 |
| 80 | -2 | -10 | -17 | -25 | -33 | -40 | -48 | -56 |
| 90 | -1 | -9 | -16 | -24 | -31 | -39 | -46 | -54 |

Figure OP4.6
An approximate guide to how wind speed reduces the temperature felt by the human body.

Once in flight, the pilot should consider actions to aid location if an emergency occurs over an area where SAR is considered especially difficult. It may be sensible to make an emergency radio call earlier than might otherwise be considered, so that the ATSU has the maximum notice that the aircraft is in difficulties and requires assistance. SAR operations will be aided if the pilot is able to pass an accurate location or if the ATSU can take a bearing on the aircraft's transmissions. The early use of the transponder emergency code may also aid location of the aircraft. If contact cannot be established with an ATSU, the pilot may choose to use the VHF distress frequency of 121.500MHz. This frequency may be monitored not only by certain ATSUs, but also by aircraft overflying 'inhospitable' areas. If a pilot hears an emergency message which is not acknowledged by an ATSU, the pilot must, if feasible, acknowledge the emergency transmission and record the position of the aircraft in distress. The pilot should inform the appropriate ATSU of the emergency transmission, giving all available information. At the pilot's discretion, while awaiting instructions, the aircraft may proceed to the position given in the emergency transmission.

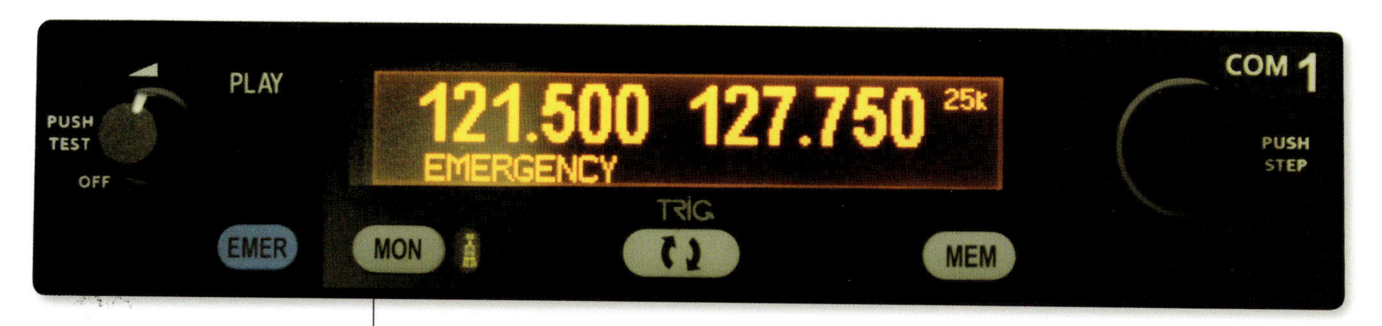


Figure OP4.7
The international VHF distress frequency is 121.500MHz.

If a Pilot In Command (PIC) sees another aircraft or a surface craft in distress, that pilot should (if possible and unless considered unreasonable or unnecessary) keep that craft in sight until compelled to leave the scene or advised that it is no longer necessary. The PIC should also determine the position of the craft in distress, report details to the appropriate ATSU, and act as instructed by the Rescue Coordination Centre (RCC) or the Air Traffic Services Unit (ATSU).

Figure OP4.8
A Search And Rescue (SAR) helicopter – in this case an S-92 'Helibus'.

Nevertheless, to prevent interference with SAR operations and to avoid an unnecessary collision hazard, pilots are strongly advised not to fly near an area where SAR operations are known to be in progress. Aircraft involved in SAR operations are likely to be performing complex manoeuvres, possibly in poor weather conditions, and the crew may not be able to maintain a good lookout for other aircraft.

## Search and rescue signals

In addition to the use of ELTs or PLBs, plus handheld radios (if carried) or mobile phones (if a signal can be obtained), there are various signals survivors can make to attract attention.

In the water, when craft are in the vicinity, survivors can attract attention by firing distress flares, using fluorescent marker to leave a trail in the sea, using an object with a bright flat surface to create a 'flash' from sunlight, or flashing a torch.

On land, survivors can use materials to make the aircraft as conspicuous as possible and/or keep a fire burning with smoke-generating material close to hand. In addition to attracting attention by firing distress flares, using an object with a bright flat surface to create a 'flash' or flashing a torch, there are also specific ground to air SAR signals which can be made on the ground. These signals should be made to contrast against the surface and if possible be at least 2.5m (8ft) long. The recognised ground to air SAR signals and their meanings are:

| SAR signal | Meaning |
|---|---|
| V | Require assistance |
| X | Require medical assistance |
| N | No or negative |
| Y | Yes or affirmative |
| → | Proceeding in this direction |

Figure OP4.9
The standard Search and Rescue signals to be used by survivors.

An aircraft can indicate that it has understood these ground signals by rocking its wings (by day) or flashing the landing lights or navigation lights on and off twice (at night).

## Progress check

34. What is the responsibility of a Rescue Coordination Centre (RCC)?
35. What is an example of an area in which Search And Rescue (SAR) services could be especially difficult?
36. In addition to an ELT or PLB, what survival equipment must be carried in a single engine aircraft for flight over water and beyond gliding distance of land?
37. In addition to an ELT or PLB, what survival equipment must be carried for flight over water and beyond gliding distance of land?

These questions are intended to test knowledge and reinforce some of the key learning points from this section. In answering these questions, a 'pass rate' of around 80% should be the target.

Model answers are found at pages 100-101.

Intentionally Left Blank

# OP5 Accidents and Incidents

Accident definitions and investigation

Safety reporting

Safety publications

Progress check

# OP5 Accidents and Incidents

## Accident definitions and investigation

The exact requirements for reporting and investigating an aircraft accident tend to be a matter of state law, but the majority of states generally follow ICAO recommendations with regard to what constitutes an accident and who should investigate it.

According to ICAO, an **aircraft accident** is an occurrence which takes place between the time any person boards the aircraft with the intention of flight, until such time as all such persons have disembarked, leading to one or more of the following events:

| Occurrence | Detail | Exceptions |
|---|---|---|
| A person is fatally or seriously injured, | as a result of being in the aircraft, or direct contact with any part of the aircraft, including parts which have become detached from the aircraft, or direct exposure to jet blast. | *Except* when the injuries are from natural causes, self-inflicted or inflicted by other persons, or when the injuries are to stowaways hiding outside the areas normally available to the passengers and crew. |
| The aircraft sustains damage or structural failure, | which adversely affects the structural which adversely affects the structural strength, performance or flight characteristics of the aircraft, and would normally require major repair or replacement of the affected component. | *Except* for engine failure or damage, when the damage is limited to a single engine, (including its cowlings or accessories), to propellers, wing tips, antennas, probes, vanes, tyres, brakes, wheels, fairings, panels, landing gear doors, windscreens, the aircraft skin (such as small dents or puncture holes) or minor damages to main rotor blades, tail rotor blades, landing gear, and those resulting from hail or bird strike, (including holes in the radome). |
| The aircraft is missing or is completely inaccessible. | | |

Figure OP5.1
Definitions of an aircraft accident.

*'Serious injury'* is defined as an injury which is sustained by a person in an accident and which:

- requires hospitalisation for more than 48 hours; or
- results in a fracture of a significant bone; or
- involves lacerations which cause severe haemorrhage, nerve, muscle or tendon damage; or
- involves injury to any internal organ; or
- involves second or third degree burns; or
- involves exposure to infectious substances or harmful radiation.

Responsibility for investigating an accident lies with the State in whose territory the accident takes place. According to ICAO:

> *"The sole objective of the investigation of an accident or incident shall be the prevention of accidents and incidents. It is not the purpose of this activity to apportion blame or liability."*

Most states have an organisation dedicated to investigating civil aviation accidents, details of which will be notified in the state's AIP. In due course, the results of the accident investigation will be published and depending on the nature of the accident, the accident report can be very detailed indeed. Nevertheless, it is notable that these reports do not identify individuals and most pilots would agree that accident reports are usually painstakingly prepared, accurate and unbiased. Accident reports are freely accessible (usually via the investigating organisation's website) and for most pilots, accident reports are almost required reading, not least because almost any accident report contains valuable information and safety lessons for other pilots. Or, as the author's first flying instructor once put it,

> *"You should learn from the mistakes of others, you won't live long enough to make them all yourself'*.

Responsibility for reporting an accident normally rests with the Pilot-In-Command (PIC) or, if the PIC is unable to do so, the aircraft operator.

## Safety reporting

Notifying and investigating accidents has obvious benefits for aviation safety, however it has been estimated that for every aircraft accident, there are probably at least 30 'incidents'. An incident is defined as *"an occurrence, other than an accident, associated with the operation of an aircraft which affects or could affect the safety of operation."*

In practice, there may be very little difference in the circumstances of an accident or a serious incident, other than the outcome. For this reason, it has become widely recognised that better information on incidents can help prevent accidents and generally improve aviation safety.

Aviation legislation sets out circumstances in which the Pilot-In-Command is required to report an incident – a process known as '**mandatory reporting**'. Occurrences which must be reported are those which may represent a significant risk to aviation safety, including occurrences related to the operation of aircraft such as:

- collision-related occurrences;
- take-off and landing-related occurrences;
- fuel-related occurrences;
- in-flight occurrences;
- communication-related occurrences;
- occurrences related to injury, emergencies and other critical situations;
- crew incapacitation and other crew-related occurrences;
- meteorological conditions or security-related occurrences.

An **occurrence** means any safety-related event which endangers or could endanger an aircraft, its occupants or any other person.

States are required to establish a Mandatory Occurrence Reporting (MOR) system to collect these reports and the Pilot-In-Command is required to report an occurrence within 72 hours of becoming aware of it, unless exceptional circumstances prevent this. It is worth knowing that safety reporting legislation requires that any personal details contained in an occurrence report (such as a person's name and address) are not recorded in national or

European databases. Indeed, the elements of a mandatory report which are available publically do not normally contain information that would allow specific aircraft or specific operators to be identified, let alone an individual. The legislation also requires that information in an occurrence report must not be made available or used in order to attribute blame or liability, nor for any purpose other than the maintenance or improvement of aviation safety.

Occurrence reporting regulations set out specific occurrences relating to 'other than complex motor powered aircraft' which must be reported. These occurrences are:

Figure OP5.2
Definitions of general aviation 'occurrences' which require reporting.

| | |
|---|---|
| **Air operations** | (1) Unintentional loss of control.<br>(2) Landing outside of intended landing area.<br>(3) Inability or failure to achieve required aircraft performance in normal conditions during take-off, climb or landing.<br>(4) Runway incursion.<br>(5) Runway excursion.<br>(6) Any flight with an aircraft which was not airworthy, or for which flight preparation was not completed, which has or could have endangered the aircraft, its occupants or any other person.<br>(7) Unintended flight into IMC (Instrument Meteorological Conditions) conditions by an aircraft not IFR (Instrument Flight Rules) certified, or a pilot not qualified for IFR, which has or could have endangered the aircraft, its occupants or any other person.<br>(8) Unintentional release of cargo. |
| **Technical occurrences** | (1) Abnormal severe vibration (for example: aileron or elevator 'flutter', or of propeller).<br>(2) Any flight control not functioning correctly or disconnected.<br>(3) A failure or substantial deterioration of the aircraft structure.<br>(4) A loss of any part of the aircraft structure or installation in flight.<br>(5) A failure of an engine, rotor, propeller, fuel system or other essential system.<br>(6) Leakage of any fluid which resulted in a fire hazard or possible hazardous contamination of aircraft structure, systems or equipment, or risk to occupants. |
| **Interaction with air navigation services and air traffic management** | (1) Interaction with air navigation services (for example: incorrect services provided, conflicting communications or deviation from clearance) which has or could have endangered the aircraft, its occupants or any other person.<br>(2) Airspace infringement. |
| **Emergencies and other critical situations** | (1) Any occurrence leading to an emergency call.<br>(2) Fire, explosion, smoke, toxic gases or toxic fumes in the aircraft.<br>(3) Incapacitation of the pilot leading to inability to perform any duty. |
| **External environment and meteorology** | (1) A collision on the ground or in the air, with another aircraft, terrain or obstacle.<br>(2) A near collision, on the ground or in the air, with another aircraft, terrain or obstacle, requiring an emergency avoidance manoeuvre to avoid a collision.<br>(3) Wildlife strike including bird strike which resulted in damage to the aircraft or loss or malfunction of any essential service.<br>(4) Interference with the aircraft by firearms, fireworks, kites, lasers, Remotely Piloted Aircraft Systems, model aircraft or by similar means.<br>(5) A lightning strike resulting in damage to, or loss of functions of, the aircraft.<br>(6) Severe turbulence encounter which resulted in injury to aircraft occupants or the need for a post-flight turbulence damage check of the aircraft.<br>(7) Icing including carburettor icing which has, or could have, endangered the aircraft, its occupants or any other person. |

Figure OP5.3
Reporting your incident may help another pilot avoid an accident.

In addition to reports by pilots concerning the operation of aircraft, reports are also required from other relevant personnel in relation to occurrences related to the condition, maintenance and repair of aircraft; occurrences related to air navigation services (eg ATC) and occurrences related to aerodromes and ground services.

Occurrence reports are treated confidentially to encourage full and free reporting from the aviation community and to protect the identity of individuals in accordance with the applicable legislation. The information which is published on specific occurrences can identify specific hazards and occurrence reports from a number of states may be collated and analysed to look for wider safety issues or dangers.

In addition to mandatory occurrence reporting systems, many organisations such as aircraft operators and sporting aviation bodies have voluntary reporting schemes which work in a similar way. Information gathered from such voluntary schemes can been used to set-up highly effective safety and information campaigns and there are a number of instances where such safety campaigns have led to a measurable improvements to safety and reductions in certain types of accident.

For a safety reporting system to work, of course, pilots must be prepared to make reports. While legislation places a specific duty on the pilot to report certain incidents, it is only human nature that a pilot may be reluctant to make a report, especially if pilot error or misjudgement is involved. There may also be a sense that the incident was a 'one-off', unlikely to reoccur. Nevertheless, just as there are very few new accidents, so there are very few new incidents and the data collected from such reports, both individually and collectively, can prevent accidents and save lives. It is worth repeating the dry words of the occurrence reporting legislation:

> *"The objective of the exchange of information on occurrences should be the prevention of aviation accidents and incidents."*

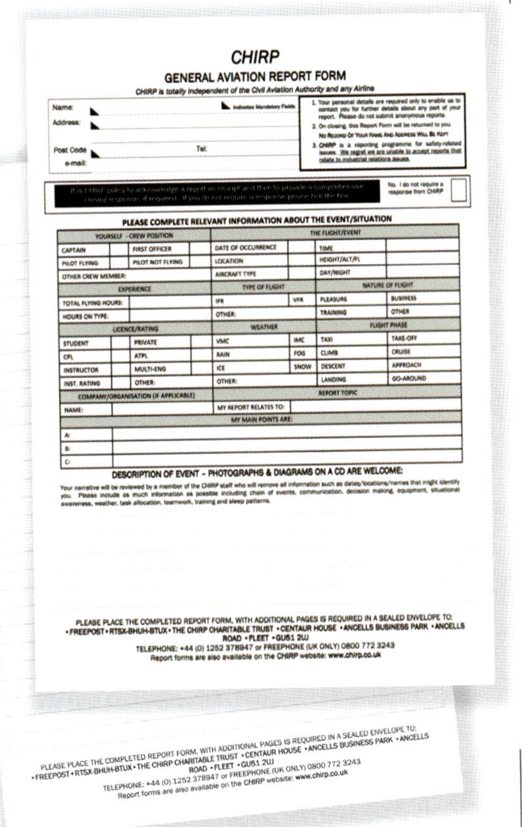

*CHIRP*

**GENERAL AVIATION REPORT FORM**

*CHIRP is totally independent of the Civil Aviation Authority and any Airline*

Name: ◣ Indicates Mandatory Fields
Address: ◣
Post Code ◣ Tel:
e-mail:

1. Your personal details are required only to enable us to contact you for further details about any part of your report. Please do not submit anonymous reports.
2. On closing, this Report Form will be returned to you. No Record Of Your Name And Address Will Be Kept
3. CHIRP is a reporting programme for safety-related issues. We regret we are unable to accept reports that relate to industrial relations issues.

It is CHIRP policy to acknowledge a report on receipt and then to provide a comprehensive closing response, if required. If you do not require a response please tick the box

No. I do not require a response from CHIRP ☐

**PLEASE COMPLETE RELEVANT INFORMATION ABOUT THE EVENT/SITUATION**

| YOURSELF - CREW POSITION | | | | THE FLIGHT/EVENT | | | |
|---|---|---|---|---|---|---|---|
| CAPTAIN | | FIRST OFFICER | | DATE OF OCCURRENCE | | TIME | |
| PILOT FLYING | | PILOT NOT FLYING | | LOCATION | | HEIGHT/ALT/FL | |
| OTHER CREW MEMBER: | | | | AIRCRAFT TYPE | | DAY/NIGHT | |
| EXPERIENCE | | | | TYPE OF FLIGHT | | NATURE OF FLIGHT | |
| TOTAL FLYING HOURS: | | | | IFR | VFR | PLEASURE | BUSINESS |
| HOURS ON TYPE: | | | | OTHER: | | TRAINING | OTHER |
| LICENCE/RATING | | | | WEATHER | | FLIGHT PHASE | |
| STUDENT | | PRIVATE | | VMC | IMC | TAXI | TAKE-OFF |
| CPL | | ATPL | | RAIN | FOG | CLIMB | CRUISE |
| INSTRUCTOR | | MULTI-ENG | | ICE | SNOW | DESCENT | APPROACH |
| INST. RATING | | OTHER: | | OTHER: | | LANDING | GO-AROUND |
| COMPANY/ORGANISATION (IF APPLICABLE) | | | | REPORT TOPIC | | | |
| NAME: | | | | MY REPORT RELATES TO: | | | |
| MY MAIN POINTS ARE: | | | | | | | |
| A: | | | | | | | |
| B: | | | | | | | |
| C: | | | | | | | |

**DESCRIPTION OF EVENT – PHOTOGRAPHS & DIAGRAMS ON A CD ARE WELCOME:**

Your narrative will be reviewed by a member of the *CHIRP* staff who will remove all information such as dates/locations/names that might identify you. Please include as much information as possible including chain of events, communication, decision making, equipment, situational awareness, weather, task allocation, teamwork, training and sleep patterns.

PLEASE PLACE THE COMPLETED REPORT FORM, WITH ADDITIONAL PAGES IS REQUIRED IN A SEALED ENVELOPE TO:
• FREEPOST • RTSX-BHUH-BTUX • THE CHIRP CHARITABLE TRUST • CENTAUR HOUSE • ANCELLS BUSINESS PARK • ANCELLS ROAD • FLEET • GU51 2UJ
TELEPHONE: +44 (0) 1252 378947 or FREEPHONE (UK ONLY) 0800 772 3243
Report forms are also available on the *CHIRP* website: www.chirp.co.uk

PLEASE PLACE THE COMPLETED REPORT FORM, WITH ADDITIONAL PAGES IS REQUIRED IN A SEALED ENVELOPE TO:
• FREEPOST • RTSX-BHUH-BTUX • THE CHIRP CHARITABLE TRUST • CENTAUR HOUSE • ANCELLS BUSINESS PARK • ANCELLS ROAD • FLEET • GU51 2UJ
TELEPHONE: +44 (0) 1252 378947 or FREEPHONE (UK ONLY) 0800 772 3243
Report forms are also available on the CHIRP website: www.chirp.co.uk

Figure OP5.4
A form used for making a confidential aviation safety report.

## Safety publications

The value of reading accident reports has already been highlighted and many pilots make a point of reading accident reports particularly when they involve aircraft types or airfields the pilot is familiar with. The organisation responsible for investigating civil aviation accidents in a state will also investigate serious incidents. A **serious incident** is an incident involving circumstances indicating that an accident nearly occurred. Examples of serious incidents (this is not a definitive list) include:

- Near collisions.
- Controlled flight into terrain (CFIT) only marginally avoided.
- Take-off or landing incidents.
- Aborted take-offs, take-offs or landings on a closed or occupied runway.
- Runway incursion.
- Gross failure to achieve predicted performance during take-off or initial climb.
- Fire in the aircraft.
- Aircraft structural failure or engine disintegration not classified as an accident.
- Flight crew incapacitation in flight.
- Fuel quantity requiring the declaration of an emergency by the pilot.
- System failure, weather phenomena, operations outside the approved flight envelope or other occurrences which could have caused difficulties controlling the aircraft.

The information contained in reports of serious incidents can prove to be every bit as valuable as that in an accident report.

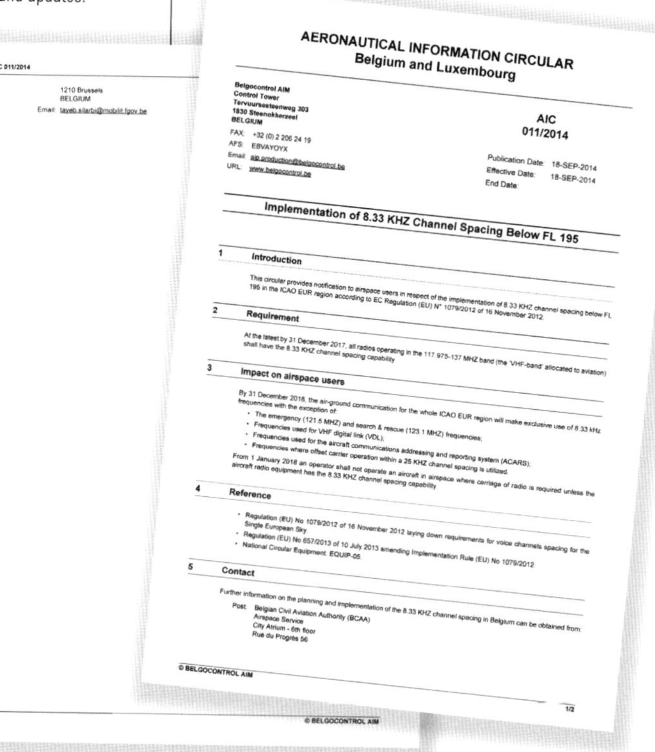

AIC 011/2014

1210 Brussels
BELGIUM

2/2

© BELGOCONTROL AIM

**AERONAUTICAL INFORMATION CIRCULAR**
**Belgium and Luxembourg**

**Belgocontrol AIM**
**Control Tower**
**Tervuursesteenweg 303**
**1830 Steenokkerzeel**
**BELGIUM**

FAX: +32 (0) 2 206 24 19
AFS: EBVAYOYX
Email: aip.production@belgocontrol.be
URL: www.belgocontrol.be

**AIC**
**011/2014**

Publication Date: 18-SEP-2014
Effective Date: 18-SEP-2014
End Date:

**Implementation of 8.33 KHZ Channel Spacing Below FL 195**

**1 Introduction**

This circular provides notification to airspace users in respect of the implementation of 8.33 KHZ channel spacing below FL 195 in the ICAO EUR region according to EC Regulation (EU) N° 1079/2012 of 16 November 2012.

**2 Requirement**

At the latest by 31 December 2017, all radios operating in the 117.975-137 MHZ band (the 'VHF-band' allocated to aviation) shall have the 8.33 KHZ channel spacing capability.

**3 Impact on airspace users**

By 31 December 2018, the air-ground communication for the whole ICAO EUR region will make exclusive use of 8.33 kHz frequencies with the exception of:

- The emergency (121.5 MHZ) and search & rescue (123.1 MHZ) frequencies;
- Frequencies used for VHF digital link (VDL);
- Frequencies used for the aircraft communications addressing and reporting system (ACARS);
- Frequencies where offset carrier operation within a 25 KHZ channel spacing is utilized.

From 1 January 2018 an operator shall not operate an aircraft in airspace where carriage of radio is required unless the aircraft radio equipment has the 8.33 KHZ channel spacing capability.

**4 Reference**

- Regulation (EU) No 1079/2012 of 16 November 2012 laying down requirements for voice channels spacing for the Single European Sky.
- Regulation (EU) No 657/2013 of 10 July 2013 amending Implementation Rule (EU) No 1079/2012.
- National Circular Equipment: EQUIP-05.

**5 Contact**

Further information on the planning and implementation of the 8.33 KHZ channel spacing in Belgium can be obtained from:

Post: Belgian Civil Aviation Authority (BCAA)
Airspace Service
City Atrium - 6th floor
Rue du Progrès 56

© BELGOCONTROL AIM

1/2

Figure OP5.5
Aeronautical Information Circulars may contain safety-related information and updates.

The competent authority may publish compilations of occurrence reports. By their nature these tend to contain less information and may be summarised compared to accident reports, but they are still a very valuable source of safety information. Occurrence and incident reports may include reports from engineers and air traffic control officers which may offer a different perspective to that a pilot normally considers.

A state may publish **Aeronautical Information Circulars (AIC)** as part of an Integrated Aeronautical Information Package (IAIP). Some of these AICs may contain information and advice on specific aspects of aviation safety and may contain valuable and useful material. Individual states may also publish safety information in their own formats, usually accessible via the competent authority's website.

Many states also publish General Aviation-specific safety information which is accessible via the website for their Competent Authority. Flying is, after-all, a global activity and it is rare for a safety hazard or issue to be confined to one state alone.

There are numerous other sources of aviation safety publications and information, including association websites, magazines and newsletters; safety promotional material from authorities and manufacturers; safety organisations and charities; and safety reports and information in General Aviation magazines. Thanks to the internet virtually all this information is available free of charge, the situation is likely to be more one of information overload than not being able to access data, guidance and advice. The most important aspect of all these excellent resources is simply to use them. It is only common sense that a pilot who reads safety publications and makes use of aviation safety resources is likely to be a more knowledgeable, better prepared and safer pilot than one who thinks he or she has nothing to learn. The most avid readers of safety publications are often the most qualified and experienced pilots.

Figure OP5.6
A General Aviation safety promotion leaflet.

Figure OP5.7
There is no shortage of aviation safety publications, many of which are dedicated to General Aviation and supported by aviation authorities and regulators.

## Progress check

38. Who is responsible for reporting an aircraft accident?
39. According to ICAO, what is the sole objective of the investigation of an aircraft accident?
40. Under mandatory reporting rules, what is an 'occurrence'?
41. If an aircraft suffers an unintentional loss of control, is the pilot required to report this occurrence?

These questions are intended to test knowledge and reinforce some of the key learning points from this section. In answering these questions, a 'pass rate' of around 80% should be the target.

Model answers are found at page 101.

# OP6 Care of Passengers

Passenger briefing and passenger procedures

Progress check

# OP6 Care of Passengers

## Passenger briefing and passenger procedures

Possibly one of the greatest responsibilities for any pilot is that of becoming entirely responsible for the care and safety of passengers. Passengers are, after-all, putting their lives and their complete trust in the hands of their pilot, and it is a foolish or reckless pilot who does not take that responsibility extremely seriously.

Figure OP6.1a
The 'airside' of any airfield, even the smallest airstrip, can be an unfamiliar and even potentially dangerous place for passengers.

Figure OP6.1b

Figure OP6.2
Passengers should normally be supervised and escorted on the 'airside' of an airfield and in and around an aircraft

Operating the aircraft safely is, of course, the primary task of the pilot and the most important element in the passenger's safety. However, in addition there are certain key additional actions the pilot can take to ensure the safety and comfort of passengers.

It is sometimes easy to forget that the 'airside' of an airfield, even a small one, can be an unfamiliar and even dangerous place for a non-pilot, so it is normally prudent to escort passengers to and from the aircraft. It is also important to remember that the features of the aircraft itself may be completely unknown to a passenger. Inexperienced passengers are at particular risk of walking into wing tips or propeller blades, trying to stand-up under a high-wing or accidentally knocking tubes and struts, unless they are carefully guided around the aircraft. If entry to the aircraft involves stepping onto the wing, passengers will need to be instructed as to where they can and cannot stand and walk. They will also need to be shown what can and cannot be used as a handhold.

Figure OP6.3a
It is rarely obvious to a novice passenger how to enter and exit a General Aviation aircraft

Figure OP6.3b

Figure OP6.4a

Figure OP6.4b

Figure OP6.4c

If entry and exit from the aircraft involves walking on the wing, passengers will need to know where they can, and cannot, stand

Figure OP6.5a

Passengers should be discouraged from pushing, pulling or moving parts of the aircraft

Figure OP6.5b

Figure OP6.6a

Extremities of the aircraft such as wing tips, tubes, struts etc. can be a hazard to the unwary

Figure OP6.6b

Once inside the cabin, passengers will need to be directed as to where they can sit and where to stow any baggage or belongings. Most pilots will have had the experience of travelling on a commercial flight and watching many of their fellow passengers blatantly ignoring the safety briefing by the cabin crew. In an average light aircraft, where there are no cabin crew to assist passengers, the passenger briefing definitely needs to be listened to! Part-NCO requires the Pilot-In-Command to ensure that before or – where appropriate during – the flight, passengers are given a **passenger briefing** on emergency equipment and procedures. These procedures should include basics such as how to put on, adjust and release the seat belts, how to open the normal exits and any emergency exits, and how to put on and adjust any headsets they may be using. Passengers must also be fully briefed on the use of any safety equipment carried – for example lifejackets – and the location of any specific items of safety equipment such as the first aid kit (and the sick bags, just in case). It may also be prudent to remind passengers not to touch any of the controls unless the pilot specifically invites them to (something that should be approached with some care in any event – just ask any flight instructor!).

Part-NCO specifically requires that, *"The Pilot-In-Command shall ensure that before or, where appropriate, during the flight, passengers are given a briefing on emergency equipment and procedures."* The guidance material to Part NCO recommends that the passenger briefing should include the locations and use of seat belts and if applicable:

(1) emergency exits;

(2) passenger emergency briefing cards;

(3) lifejackets;

(4) oxygen dispensing equipment;

(5) life rafts; and

(6) other emergency equipment provided for individual passenger use.

The briefing should also include the location and use of the principal emergency equipment carried for collective use.

Passengers also need to understand that they should not talk to or otherwise distract the pilot at certain key times, such as before and during take-off and landing, or when the pilot is listening to radio communications (the latter is not always clear to passengers, who often have an extraordinary ability to start talking the very moment the pilot starts listening to an important radio message).

Part-NCO specifies that the PIC must ensure that, prior to and during taxiing, take-off and landing, and whenever deemed necessary in the interest of safety, *"each passenger on board occupies a seat or berth and has his/her safety belt or restraint device properly secured."*

When carrying passengers, Part-NCO requires that the PIC must not simulate:

- situations that require the use of abnormal or emergency procedures; or
- flight in Instrument Meteorological Conditions (IMC).

During the flight the pilot will need to regularly check on the welfare of the passengers, making sure that they are comfortable and content and remembering not to manoeuvre too energetically, especially with a nervous passenger who may find steep angles of bank particularly unnerving. Before landing the pilot needs to double check that everyone on board, and their baggage, is properly secured as part of the pre-landing checks. At the end of the flight, passengers are likely to need further guidance on how to safely disembark the aircraft and leave the 'airside'.

Figure OP6.7a
The aircraft propeller, whether stationary or turning, can be surprisingly difficult to see.

Figure OP6.7b

As a general rule, the non-commercial operation of aircraft assumes that the pilot decides where and when to fly and is solely responsible for the costs of the flying he or she undertakes. However, the Part-NCO regulations do allow 'cost sharing' between a pilot and passengers for non-commercial flights. As you might expect, there are some specific provisions for cost sharing, in particular:

- The aircraft must be a non-complex ('other-than-complex') type;
- There can be no more than six aircraft occupants, including the pilot;
- Costs must be shared amongst all the occupants (including the pilot), although there is no requirement that costs are shared equally;
- Only direct costs can be shared – for example aircraft rental, fuel, landing fees.

There must be no element of profit in the cost-sharing process, and aviation authorities are very concerned to make sure that passengers are not flown in some sort of 'air taxi' or 'commercial' sense under the pretence of cost-sharing. In practice, the interpretation of cost-sharing rules varies between different states and it is sensible to check the national interpretation of the rules before making a cost-sharing arrangement. As with so many areas of aviation, if a proposed operation seems dubious, or involves 'bending the rules' in some way, that's a good sign that it's a bad idea.

Part-NCO rules also allow certain other activities (such as introductory flights, parachute dropping, sailplane towing or aerobatic flights) to be conducted as non-commercial flights, but with further rules regarding the organisations organising the flights. Some element of remuneration or valuable consideration is also allowed for air display and competition flying, but again checking the national interpretation of the rules is wise.

None of the tasks involved in passenger care should be too onerous or demanding, but they do need additional consideration, especially the first few times the pilot carries passengers. The various aspects of passenger care all take time, so the pilot should be mindful of the additional time required for looking after passengers when planning the flight. The extra attention needed for passengers, especially inexperienced ones, should also be a consideration if the planned flight is likely to be particularly challenging or complex. It may be better to change the planned flight or leave the carriage of passengers for another day.

Nonetheless, all of these safety considerations should not make a pilot reluctant to take passengers flying other than for safety reasons. Sharing a passion for flying with others is one of the great pleasures and privileges of holding a pilot licence. Who knows, maybe some of your passengers are potential pilots themselves?

## Progress check

42. Which person carries the primary responsibility for the safety of passengers on-board an aircraft?
43. Is a passenger briefing required in a light aircraft on non-commercial operations?
44. When are passengers required to fasten their seat-belt?

These questions are intended to test knowledge and reinforce some of the key learning points from this section. In answering these questions, a 'pass rate' of around 80% should be the target.

Model answers are found at page 101.

Intentionally Left Blank

# OP7 National Procedures

National rules and procedures

Progress check

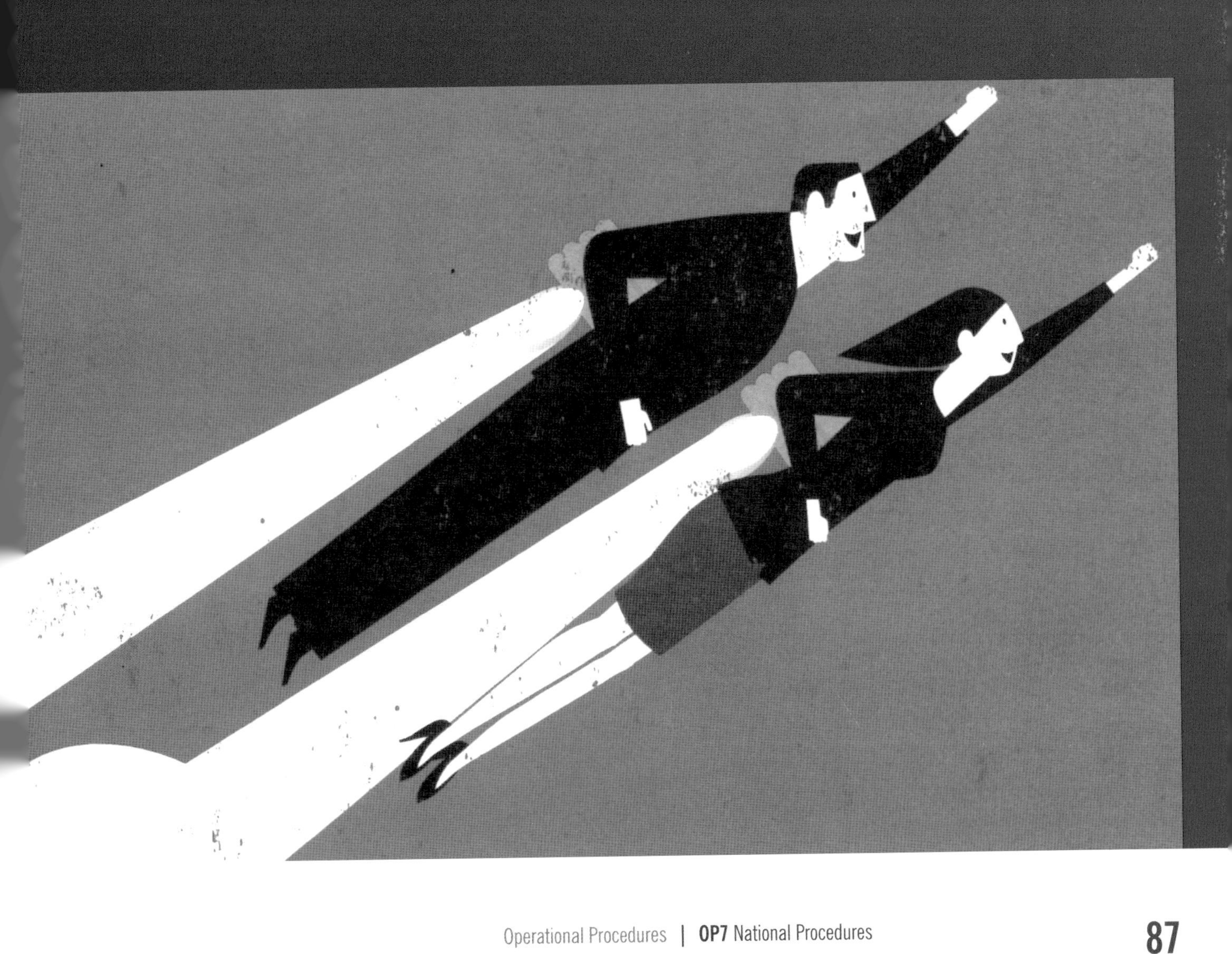

# OP7 National Procedures

## National rules and procedures

The following information applies specifically to the United Kingdom (UK), which for the purposes of this publication consists of England, Wales, Scotland and Northern Ireland. It should be noted that some territories that might normally be considered to be part of the UK, such as the Channel Islands and the Isle of Man, have their own aviation legislation.

When the UK left the European Aviation Safety Agency (EASA) at the end of 2020, the existing EU legislation was taken into UK law automatically. It follows that the following information in relation to UK rules and procedures is limited to those elements which are significantly different to the EU/EASA or ICAO procedures already covered. The following UK-specific information is presented under the same chapter headings as used in sections OP1 – OP6.

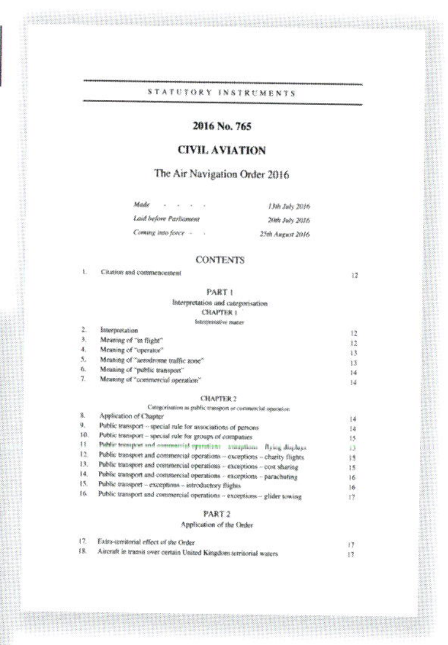

STATUTORY INSTRUMENTS

**2016 No. 765**

**CIVIL AVIATION**

The Air Navigation Order 2016

| | |
|---|---|
| *Made - - - -* | *13th July 2016* |
| *Laid before Parliament* | *20th July 2016* |
| *Coming into force - -* | *25th August 2016* |

CONTENTS

1. Citation and commencement 12

PART 1
Interpretation and categorisation
CHAPTER 1
Interpretative matter

2. Interpretation 12
3. Meaning of "in flight" 12
4. Meaning of "operator" 13
5. Meaning of "aerodrome traffic zone" 13
6. Meaning of "public transport" 14
7. Meaning of "commercial operation" 14

CHAPTER 2
Categorisation as public transport or commercial operation

8. Application of Chapter 14
9. Public transport – special rule for associations of persons 14
10. Public transport – special rule for groups of companies 15
11. Public transport and commercial operations – exceptions – flying displays 15
12. Public transport and commercial operations – exceptions – charity flights 15
13. Public transport and commercial operations – exceptions – cost sharing 15
14. Public transport and commercial operations – exceptions – parachuting 16
15. Public transport – exceptions – introductory flights 16
16. Public transport and commercial operations – exceptions – glider towing 17

PART 2
Application of the Order

17. Extra-territorial effect of the Order 17
18. Aircraft in transit over certain United Kingdom territorial waters 17

Figure OP7.1

The UK Air Navigation Order (ANO).

### Operation of aircraft

In the UK, regulations concerning the operation of non-Part 21 aircraft are contained within the Air Navigation Order (ANO). The ANO also establishes general safety requirements applicable to all aircraft in UK airspace and people involved in aircraft operations.

The Air Navigation Order contains specific provisions regarding the **Pilot-In-Command**, meaning the pilot designated by the operator as being in command and charged with the safe conduct of its flight, without being under the direction of any other pilot in the aircraft.

The ANO goes into considerable detail on the obligations of the Pilot-In-Command, presented in a series of sections.

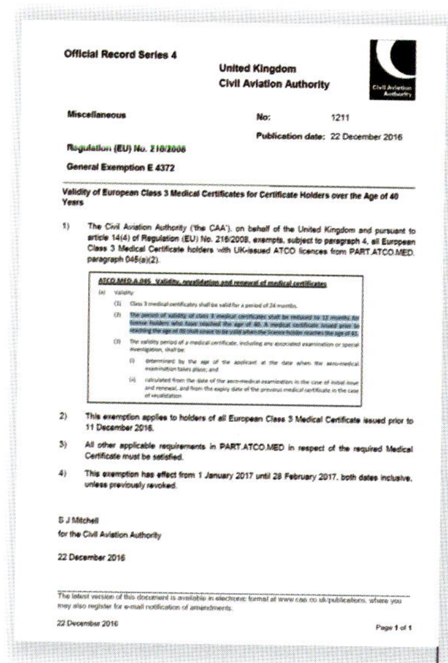

**Official Record Series 4**

**United Kingdom**
**Civil Aviation Authority**



**Miscellaneous**

**No:** 1211

**Publication date:** 22 December 2016

**Regulation (EU) No. 216/2008**

**General Exemption E 4372**

**Validity of European Class 3 Medical Certificates for Certificate Holders over the Age of 40 Years**

1) The Civil Aviation Authority ('the CAA'), on behalf of the United Kingdom and pursuant to article 14(4) of Regulation (EU) No. 216/2008, exempts, subject to paragraph 4, all European Class 3 Medical Certificate holders with UK-issued ATCO licences from PART.ATCO.MED. paragraph 045(a)(2).

> ATCO.MED.A.045 Validity, revalidation and renewal of medical certificates
> (a) Validity
> (1) Class 3 medical certificates shall be valid for a period of 24 months.
> (2) The period of validity of class 3 medical certificates shall be reduced to 12 months for licence holders who have reached the age of 40. A medical certificate issued prior to reaching the age of 40 shall cease to be valid when the licence holder reaches the age of 41.
> (3) The validity period of a medical certificate, including any associated examination or special investigation, shall be:
> (i) determined by the age of the applicant at the date when the aero-medical examination takes place; and
> (ii) calculated from the date of the aero-medical examination in the case of initial issue and renewal, and from the expiry date of the previous medical certificate in the case of revalidation.

2) This exemption applies to holders of all European Class 3 Medical Certificate issued prior to 11 December 2016.

3) All other applicable requirements in PART.ATCO.MED in respect of the required Medical Certificate must be satisfied.

4) This exemption has effect from 1 January 2017 until 28 February 2017, both dates inclusive, unless previously revoked.

S J Mitchell
for the Civil Aviation Authority

22 December 2016

The latest version of this document is available in electronic format at www.caa.co.uk/publications, where you may also register for e-mail notification of amendments.

22 December 2016 Page 1 of 1

Figure OP7.2

'ORS4' notices from the CAA tend to contain temporary exemptions to aviation legislation.

*Aerodromes*

The Pilot-In-Command must only use aerodromes and operating sites that are adequate for the type of aircraft and operation.

*Flight preparation*

Before commencing a flight, the Pilot-In-Command must determine by every reasonable means available that surface facilities, including communication and navigation aids available and directly required for the safe operation of the aircraft, are adequate for the type of operation planned.

*Take-off and landing conditions*

Before commencing take-off, the Pilot-In-Command must be satisfied that, according to the information available, the weather at the aerodrome or operating site and the condition of the runway and take-off area intended to be used will not prevent a safe take-off and departure.

Before commencing an approach to land, the Pilot-In-Command must be satisfied that, according to the information available, the weather at the aerodrome or the operating site and the condition of the runway or final approach and area intended to be used will not prevent a safe approach, landing or missed approach.

*Operating procedures*
The Pilot-In-Command must ensure that the flight is performed in such a way that the operating procedures specified in the flight manual or, where required the operations manual, are followed; and procedures are established and followed for any reasonably foreseeable emergency situation. An operations manual is a document which may be prepared by the aircraft operator containing advice and instructions about the operation of the aircraft, additional to the information contained in the Aircraft Flight Manual (AFM).

*Meteorological conditions*
The Pilot-In-Command must only commence or continue a Visual Flight Rules (VFR) flight if the latest available meteorological information indicates that the weather conditions along the route and at the intended destination at the estimated time of use will be at or above the applicable Visual Flight Rules operating minima. Additionally, the Pilot-In-Command must have planned an alternative course of action for the eventuality that the flight cannot be completed as planned because of weather conditions.

*Airworthiness, equipment, baggage and cargo*
The Pilot-In-Command must ensure that the aircraft is airworthy; *that* instruments and equipment required for the flight are installed in the aircraft and are operative, (unless operation with inoperative or missing equipment is permitted by the minimum equipment list or the CAA); and that all equipment, baggage and cargo are properly loaded and secured and that an emergency evacuation of the aircraft remains possible.

*Mass and balance*
The Pilot-In-Command must ensure that during any phase of operation, the loading, the mass and the centre of gravity position of the aircraft comply with any limitations specified in the Aircraft Flight Manual (AFM).and the weight schedule (if required), or equivalent document.

*Fuel, oil and ballast*
The Pilot-In-Command must ensure sufficient fuel, oil and engine coolant (if required) are carried for the intended flight, and that a safe margin has been allowed for contingencies.

During flight, the Pilot-In-Command must keep any safety belt fastened and remain at the controls of the aircraft at all times except if another pilot is taking the controls.

A person must not recklessly or negligently act in a manner likely to **endanger an aircraft**, or any person in an aircraft. A person must not recklessly or negligently cause or permit an aircraft to endanger any person or property.

A person must not enter any aircraft when drunk, or be drunk in any aircraft. A member of the crew of any aircraft must not be under the influence of drink or a drug to such an extent that it impairs their capacity.

Notices indicating when smoking is prohibited in an aircraft must be visible from each passenger seat. A person must not smoke at a time when smoking is prohibited by a notice. As a general rule, smoking is prohibited by permanent notices (or strongly discouraged) in all aircraft.

Under the ANO an aircraft must have on board those **documents** which it is required to carry under the law of the country in which it is registered. For the purposes of complying with the ANO, a private flight within the UK, a UK-registered aircraft is not required to carry any documents.

For the purposes of complying with Part-NCO, the UK CAA permit the following documents of to be left at the aerodrome or operating site if the flight is taking off and landing at the same place, or operating solely within the London and Scottish Flight Information Regions (FIR):

- the original certificate of registration (C of R);
- the original certificate of airworthiness (C of A);
- the noise certificate (if applicable);
- a list of specific approvals (if applicable);
- the aircraft radio licence (if applicable);
- third party liability insurance certificate(s);
- the journey log, or equivalent, for the aircraft.

For an international private flight, a UK-registered aircraft is required to carry:

- the national certificate of airworthiness;
- the certificate of registration;
- a licence for the aircraft radio station installed in the aircraft;
- the flight crew licences;
- a copy of the national airworthiness review certificate (if required);
- the technical log (if required);
- a copy of the procedures to be followed by the Pilot-In-Command of an intercepted aircraft, and the visual signals for use by intercepting and intercepted aircraft.

The commander of an aircraft must, within a reasonable time after being requested to do so by an authorised person, produce to that authorised person:

- the certificates of registration and airworthiness for the aircraft;
- the flight crew licences, medical certificate or medical deceleration;
- any other documents which the aircraft is required to carry in flight under the ANO or an EU Regulation.

A pilot must preserve his or her flying logbook for at least two years from the date of the last entry in it, and produce it to an authorised person within a reasonable time after being requested to do so by that person. In practice, most pilots keep all their flying logbooks for life and this is strongly recommended as the pilot's logbook(s) soon become(s) the only complete record of all the flights a pilot has made.

An aircraft must not carry any **munition of war** except with the permission of the CAA. Any sporting weapon or munition of war must be carried in a place which is not accessible to passengers in flight.

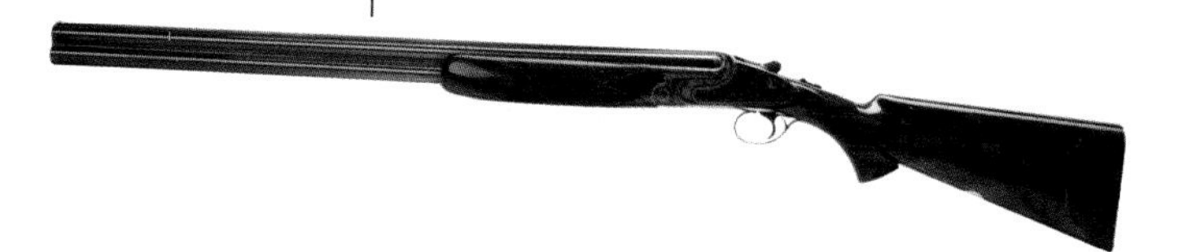

Figure OP7.3
The carriage of weapons and 'munitions of war' in a UK-registered aircraft is regulated by specific provisions of the Air Navigation Order.

An aircraft must not fly unless it is equipped to comply with the law of the country in which it is registered. An aircraft registered in the United Kingdom must carry the **equipment** specified by the ANO. An aeroplane on a private flight by day, in VMC, is required to be equipped with a means of measuring and displaying the:

- magnetic heading;
- time, in hours, minutes and seconds;
- pressure altitude;
- indicated airspeed.

Instruments and equipment used to control the flight path and required by the ANO must be approved in accordance with the applicable airworthiness requirements. Equipment approval is not needed for an accurate time piece.

Unless the CAA permit otherwise, aeroplanes must be equipped with:

- a seat or berth for each person on board who is aged 24 months or more;
- a seat belt on each passenger seat and restraining belts for each berth;
- a child restraint device for each person on board younger than 24 months; and
- a seat belt with upper torso restraint system on each flight crew seat, with a single point of release.

A child restraint device does not require any form of CAA 'approval'.

An aircraft with a UK CAA certificate of airworthiness and with a maximum take-off mass of more than 1,200kg must be equipped with at least one hand **fire extinguisher** in the flight crew compartment; and in each passenger compartment that is separate from the flight crew compartment, unless that passenger compartment is readily accessible to the flight crew.

When an aeroplane flies beyond gliding distance from land suitable for an emergency landing, or takes off or lands at an aerodrome or operating site where (in the opinion of the Pilot-In-Command), the take-off or approach path is over water and there is a likelihood of a ditching in the event of an emergency; it must be equipped with a **lifejacket** for each person on board, or equivalent individual floatation device for each person on board younger than 24 months. That lifejacket or floatation device must be worn (this is strongly recommended), or stowed where it is readily accessible from the seat or berth of the person for whom it is provided. This survival equipment does not require any form of CAA 'approval'.

A non-pressurised aircraft operating above 13,000ft must carry sufficient **oxygen and oxygen equipment** to supply all crew and passengers with oxygen for all the time the aircraft is above 13,000ft. A non-pressurised aircraft operating above 10,000ft and below 13,000ft for more than 30 minutes, must carry sufficient oxygen and oxygen equipment to supply all crew and at least 10% of the passengers with oxygen for any period in excess of 30 minutes at that level. This survival equipment does not require any form of CAA 'approval'.

In certain circumstances an aircraft on a private, VFR flight must carry specific items of **radio equipment**. A VFR flight in controlled airspace must be equipped with radio communication equipment capable of maintaining direct two-way communication with the appropriate air traffic control units on the intended route using the frequencies notified.

Aircraft operated over routes that cannot be navigated by reference to visual landmarks must be equipped with any **navigation equipment** necessary to enable them to proceed in accordance with the air traffic service flight plan (if applicable) and any applicable notified airspace requirements. Aircraft must have sufficient navigation equipment so that, in the event of the failure of one item of equipment, the remaining equipment will allow safe navigation – or an appropriate contingency action – to be completed safely.

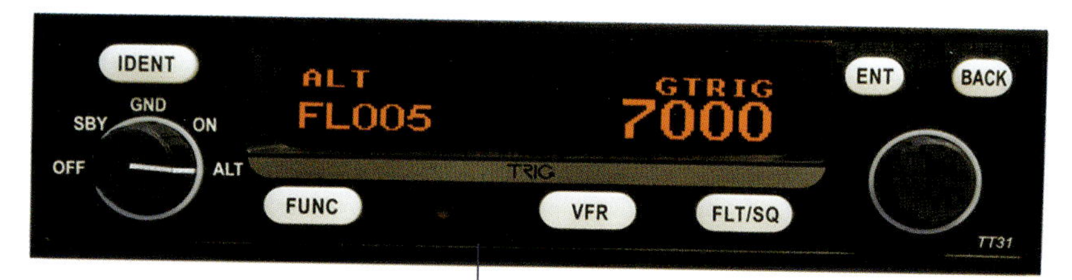


Figure OP7.4
A typical General Aviation transponder.

In Class A, B and C airspace the aircraft must also be equipped with secondary surveillance radar (SSR) equipment which includes a pressure altitude reporting **transponder** capable of operating in Mode A and Mode C and has Mode S. Additionally, there are certain areas of uncontrolled airspace where the operation of radio equipment or transponder equipment is mandatory, ie Radio Mandatory Zones (RMZ) and Transponder Mandatory Zones (TMZ). A flight above FL100 in uncontrolled airspace is required to be equipped with an SSR transponder to the same standard as for flight within Class A, B & C airspace.

**Avoidance of Hazards**

The UK CAA uses wake turbulence categories and wake turbulence separations different to Eurocontrol and ICAO recommendations. The United Kingdom conforms in general to the ICAO standards on wake turbulence but with certain modifications to the weight and separation relationship which experience has shown to be advisable for the safety of operations at UK aerodromes. Details of the current UK wake turbulence categories and separations are to be found in an Aeronautical Information Circular (AIC). The key difference to ICAO standards is the introduction of additional categories, namely 'Small' for aircraft with a Maximum Take-Off Weight (MTOW) authorised of between 40,000kg and 17,000kg and the spilt of the 'Medium' category into 'Upper Medium' (104,000kg to 136,000kg) and 'Lower Medium' (40,000kg to 104,000kg). In practice, the Upper Medium category contains a very small number of aircraft, of which the only one in regular operation in the UK is the Boeing 757.

The UK wake turbulence categories are:

| Category | MTOW |
|---|---|
| Super/Heavy | 136,000kg or more |
| Upper Medium | 104,000kg to 136,000kg |
| Lower Medium | 40,000kg to 104,000kg |
| Small | 17,000kg to 40,000kg |
| Light | less than 17,000kg |
| In the UK the SUPER category is assigned to the Airbus A380-800, Antonov AN-124 Ruslan and Antonov AN-225 Mriya | |

Figure OP7.5
The UK Wake Turbulence categories.

The UK wake turbulence separation minima on final approach are:

| Leading aircraft category | Following aircraft category | Separation |
|---|---|---|
| Super | Light | 8 nautical miles |
| Heavy | Light | 7 nautical miles |
| Upper Medium | Light | 6 nautical miles |
| Lower Medium | Light | 5 nautical miles |
| Small | Light | 4 nautical miles |
| These separation minima also apply to parallel runways, different runways and situations where the following aircraft will cross the leading aircraft's flight path at the same level or less than 1000ft below. | | |

Figure OP7.6
UK wake turbulence separation minima on final approach.

The UK wake turbulence separation minima on departure are, where the following aircraft is departing from the **same point** as leading aircraft, are:

| Leading aircraft category | Following aircraft category | Separation |
|---|---|---|
| Super | Light | 3 minutes |
| Heavy | Light | 2 minutes |
| Medium or Small | Light | 2 minutes |
| Time separation based on airborne time interval. Separation also applies to parallel runways and different runways if the following aircraft will cross the leading aircraft's flight path at the same level or less than 1000ft below. | | |

Figure OP7.7
UK wake turbulence separation minima on departure, if the following aircraft is departing from the same point as leading aircraft.

Take-off wake turbulence minima where the following aircraft is departing from an **intermediate point** from the leading aircraft, are:

| Leading aircraft category | Following aircraft category | Separation |
|---|---|---|
| Super | Light | 4 minutes |
| Heavy | Light | 3 minutes |
| Medium | Light | 3 minutes |
| Time separation is based on airborne time interval. Separation minima also apply to parallel runways and to different runways if the following aircraft will cross the leading aircraft's flight path at the same level or less than 1000ft below. | | |

Figure OP7.8
UK wake turbulence separation minima on departure, if the following aircraft is departing from an intermediate point from leading aircraft.

The UK wake turbulence AIC notes that the wake turbulence minima on departure are applied by ATC and that ATC does not have the discretion to reduce these minima.

**Search and Rescue Procedures**

UK Search and Rescue procedures are detailed in the UK AIP. The UK has not formally designated land or sea areas where SAR operations would be difficult, however the UK AIP strongly recommends that General Aviation (GA) aircraft should carry appropriate survival equipment, including an Emergency Locator Transmitter (ELT) or Personal Locator Beacon (PLB), when planning to operate over mountainous or sparsely populated areas. The UK AIP advises that certain land areas within the UK are considered to be difficult from a SAR aspect:

- The Scottish Highlands;
- The Hebrides, Orkneys and Shetlands;
- The Pennine Range;
- The Lake District;
- The Yorkshire Moors;
- The Welsh Mountains;
- The Peak District of Derbyshire;
- Exmoor;
- Dartmoor.

Figure OP7.9
Land areas of the UK considered to be difficult for Search And Rescue (SAR) operations.

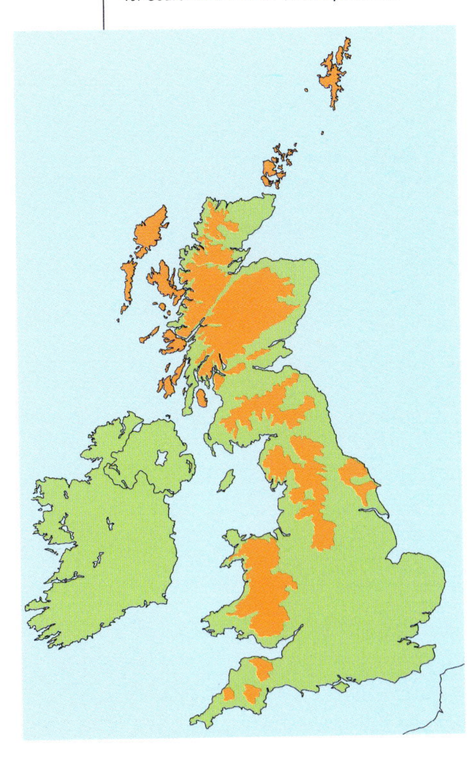

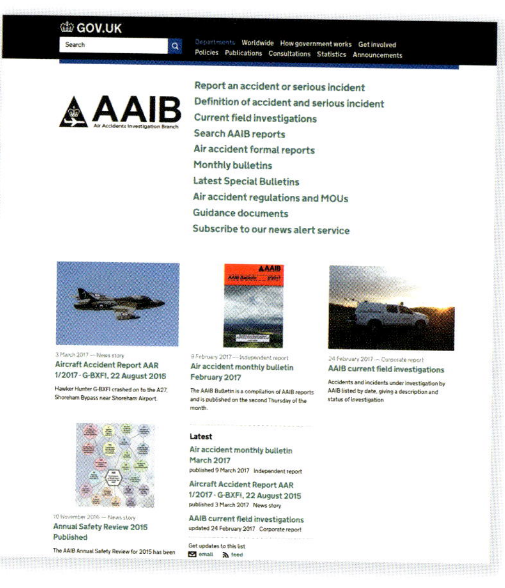


Figure OP7.10
The UK Air Accidents Investigation Branch website.

## Accidents and Incidents

In the UK the investigation of accidents and serious incidents is the role of the Air Accidents Investigation Branch (AAIB). In the event of an accident within the UK the AAIB and the police must be notified without delay by the aircraft commander, or the aircraft operator if the commander is unable to do so. Accident and serious incident reports, which do not identify individual pilots, are published in monthly bulletins available from the AAIB website.

'Occurrences' can be reported via the UK CAA website.

The PIC of an aircraft must make a report to the CAA of any birdstrike occurrence which occurs whilst the aircraft is in flight in or over the United Kingdom. 'Birdstrike occurrence' means an incident in flight in which the PIC of an aircraft has reason to believe that the aircraft has been in collision with one or more birds.

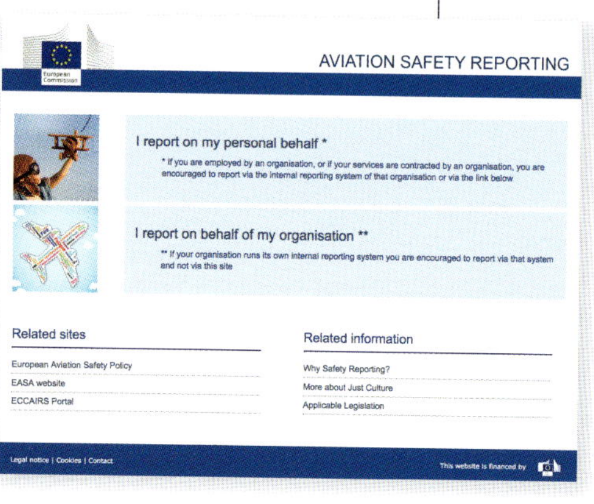


Figure OP7.11
The on-line occurrence reporting portal, accessed via the UK CAA website.

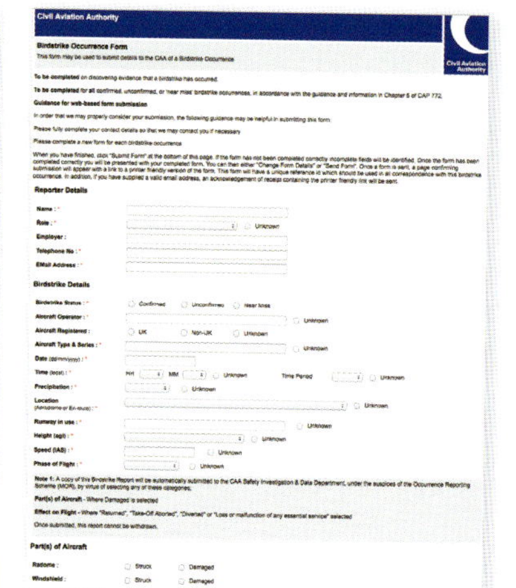


Figure OP7.12
The UK CAA has an on-line form for reporting a bird strike.

Aircraft getting too close together unintentionally is clearly a risk pilots want to avoid. An 'airprox' is defined as *"A situation in which, in the opinion of a pilot or a controller, the distance between aircraft, as well as their relative positions and speed, was such that the safety of the aircraft involved was, or may have been, compromised."*

General Aviation pilots are asked to make voluntary reports of an airprox to the UK Airprox Board (UKAB). The UKAB publish the finding of its investigations of reports on its website, which also contains valuable safety information and guidance. It is not the purpose of the UKAB to apportion blame or liability: the sole objective of each investigation is to assess a notified airprox in the interests of improving safety by identifying lessons that may be applicable to others, or policy and procedures which might be improved. All UKAB reports are dis-identified and aircraft registrations, names of companies or individuals are not released or published, in order to encourage an open and honest reporting environment.

Figure OP7.13
A form for reporting a UK 'Airprox'.

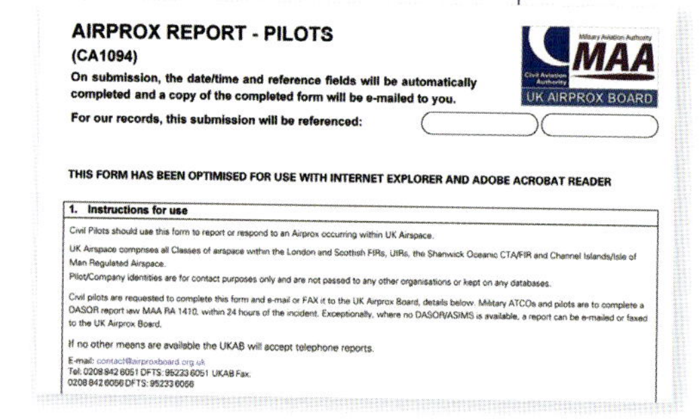

**AIRPROX REPORT - PILOTS**
**(CA1094)**
**On submission, the date/time and reference fields will be automatically completed and a copy of the completed form will be e-mailed to you.**
**For our records, this submission will be referenced:**

Military Aviation Authority MAA
Civil Aviation Authority
UK AIRPROX BOARD

**THIS FORM HAS BEEN OPTIMISED FOR USE WITH INTERNET EXPLORER AND ADOBE ACROBAT READER**

**1. Instructions for use**

Civil Pilots should use this form to report or respond to an Airprox occurring within UK Airspace.

UK Airspace comprises all Classes of airspace within the London and Scottish FIRs, UIRs, the Shanwick Oceanic CTA/FIR and Channel Islands/Isle of Man Regulated Airspace.
Pilot/Company identities are for contact purposes only and are not passed to any other organisations or kept on any databases.

Civil pilots are requested to complete this form and e-mail or FAX it to the UK Airprox Board, details below. Military ATCOs and pilots are to complete a DASOR report iaw MAA RA 1410, within 24 hours of the incident. Exceptionally, where no DASOR/ASIMS is available, a report can be e-mailed or faxed to the UK Airprox Board.

If no other means are available the UKAB will accept telephone reports.

E-mail: contact@airproxboard.org.uk
Tel: 0208 842 6051 DFTS: 95233 6051 UKAB Fax:
0208 842 6056 DFTS: 95233 6056

**CHIRP – Confidential & Independent Reporting**

alert. However I am not completely sure about this; it may be that I was focused "eyes out" at the critical moment and too focussed on the weather ahead to notice what my computers were telling me.

5. I usually fly IFR in CAS; flying VFR outside CAS, perhaps my nav thought processes are not as second nature to me as they should be.

As to what I could have done differently (in no particular order):

1. If I had checked a radar image before the flight it would have been obvious that my planned route was not going to work. I would have planned to fly further west and the issue would not have arisen. I was lulled into a false sense of security by the near perfect weather that I had been (until then) experiencing all day.

2. As soon as I realised I would not be able to cross Luton Zone I should have picked up a LARS from Farnborough, as they would likely have stopped me in my tracks. (Workload meant that I did not think to do this). I doubt a listening squawk on Luton would have helped, as they were too busy vectoring weather-avoiding aircraft on their approach to worry about GA outside of their zone.

3. On determining the need to re-route in an ad hoc way during flight, I should have been much more careful to check systematically the entire length of my proposed diversion, not least the airspace immediately in front of me.

4. Given that I was in VMC and could see the weather perfectly well out of the windscreen, I should not have distracted myself with satellite weather. I did not need it. If I had not been looking at that I would have had more spare cognitive capacity and would probably also have had the benefit of a Sky Demon alert.

5. If I had rerouted earlier (or indeed later) I would have avoided the danger area. However I see that not as something that I should have done differently but rather as a question of luck.

6. I have given careful thought to the extent that my use of electronic charting software was a causative factor. Whilst I firmly believe that tools such as Sky Demon provide a far safer, better and more reliable means of navigation than conventional map reading, I cannot deny that it may have been a contributing factor here in that had I been navigating without Sky Demon I suspect I might have spent longer reviewing the planned route and surrounding airspace when on the ground, with the result that I might have been aware of the danger area before I set off.

***CHIRP* Comment: The reporter is commended for his honesty and thorough analysis. We are delighted to print this report with only minor comments to add. If there is a listening squawk published, we would recommend using it whenever listening out on an airfield frequency. We agree completely with the reporter's suggestion that he did not need the satellite weather on his iPad while he was good VMC; when navigating manually off a planned track, aids such as Sky Demon really come into their own and a timely alert from it would likely have saved the day.**

Back to the Top

**PRE-FLIGHT CHECK FAILURE**

**Report Text:** I arrived at the airfield at midday to clean my flexwing microlight and do some local flying. My co-owner was already there having flown in the morning. To clean the wing we decided to "hobble" the aircraft. This involved removing the front strut from the trike (held in place by clevis pins and safety rings) and lowering the wing. We then cleaned the wing and applied sun protection spray. This done, we raised the wing with some little difficulty and I replaced the front strut. My co-owner then departed.

Another flying buddy had arrived and we decided to fly together to a local strip. I quickly pre-flighted the aircraft, started up and performed my pre-take off checks at the hold point. My buddy had already taken off but landed just as I was completing my checks to tell me that our planned route was looking murky, and suggested an alternative. He then took off and I followed shortly afterwards.

As the aircraft took off, I felt the control bar movement was unusual, glanced up and saw that I hadn't replaced the top clevis pin and the strut had now detached from the pylon. I performed an immediate emergency landing, made a lot simpler by having a long WWII concrete runway available straight ahead.

**CHIRP – Confidential & Independent Reporting - Page 4**

Figure OP7.14

A CHIRP GA Feedback newsletter, filled with candid safety reports.

- do not obstruct the controls with objects such as cameras, handbags, knees or feet.
- do not put metallic or magnetic objects near the compass.
- switch OFF all mobile telephones and electronic devices before flight.
- do not interfere with the controls in flight.
- know how to use the headsets.
- can use the intercom, if fitted, and know how to communicate if there is no intercom.
- know where to find the sick-bags.
- know the emergency procedures detailed below.

5 **EMERGENCIES**

a) Before flight, the pilot must brief passengers on how to brace themselves if a forced landing or ditching appears likely. There are two main reasons for this:

- To reduce injury due to striking objects inside the aircraft.
- To reduce 'flailing' of the body.

b) Passengers in forward-facing seats WITHOUT a control wheel/stick in front of them should, if possible, be briefed to adopt the 'brace' position. The upper body should be bent forward as far as possible with the chest close to the thighs and knees and the head touching the back of the seat in front. The hands should be placed one on top of the other on top of the head with the forearms tucked in against the side of the face. Fingers should NOT be interlocked. The lower legs should be inclined aft of the vertical with the feet flat on the floor. The seat belt should be as tight as possible and low on the torso.

c) Check that front seat occupants have got their belt and upper torso restraint as tight as possible prior to impact.

d) Advise passengers how to use any emergency exits. Tell them to kick or force out a window if the doors or canopy cannot be opened or if the aircraft has overturned.

e) Remind rear seat passengers how to operate the seat-back release on the front seats (thus allowing rear seat passengers to vacate the aircraft).

f) Agree the order in which the aircraft should be evacuated.

g) Remind passengers that harnesses and belts should be as tight as possible and at the last minute headsets removed, unplugged and stowed.

Figure OP7.15

The UK CAA publish a series of 'Safety Sense' leaflets, all available to download free of charge from the UK CAA website.

The UK also operates a **Confidential Human Factors Incident Reporting Programme** for aviation – known as 'CHIRP'. CHIRP provides a totally independent and confidential reporting system for all individuals employed in or associated with the aviation industry. By using CHIRP, individuals are able to raise safety-related issues without being identified to other pilots, management, or the CAA. CHIRP publishes a quarterly newsletter of GA-related reports called CHIRP GA FEEDBACK.

THE UK CAA issue various safety-related publications including Aeronautical Information Circulars (AIC), pink-series AICs are specifically safety-related. The UK CAA also publish a series of 'Safety Sense' leaflets, together with 'Handling Sense' leaflets and GA Safety Posters, all of which relate to a particular area of GA safety.

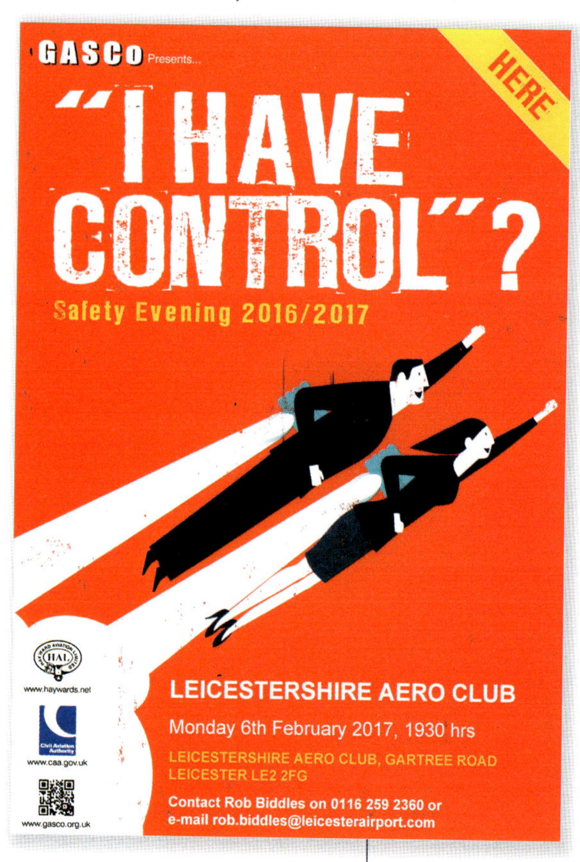


Figure OP7.16

GASCo safety evenings are an excellent opportunity to update your knowledge, gain valuable safety insights and meet fellow pilots.

In the UK there is a charitable organisation known as **GASCo** (General Aviation Safety Council), who publish a quarterly GA safety magazine ('GASCo Flight Safety') and monthly e-mail newsletters ('Flight Safety Extra') as well as hosting an aviation safety website. GASCo also organise regular 'Safety Evenings' around the UK at which a range of safety-related topics are discussed and safety information given out. A study made some years ago concluded that pilots who had attended a safety evening were significantly less likely to be involved in an accident than those who had not. The lesson is probably not that safety evenings have some magic effect on pilots, but rather that a pilot who wants to know more about aviation safety and keep on learning has a mind-set and approach to flying that makes that person a better, safer, pilot.

### Care of Passengers

The ANO states that the Pilot-In-Command (PIC) must ensure that passengers are given a briefing on emergency equipment and procedures before (or where appropriate) during the flight.

If the planned flight will exceed 13,000ft altitude in an un-pressurised aircraft, before (or where appropriate during) the flight, passengers must be given a briefing on use of supplemental oxygen. The PIC must also ensure that the pilot and flight crew members engaged in performing essential duties use supplemental oxygen continuously whenever the cabin altitude exceeds:

- 10,000 feet for a period of more than 30 minutes; or
- 13,000 feet.

Whenever the cabin altitude exceeds 13,000 feet, all passengers are recommended to use supplemental oxygen.

The Pilot-In-Command must ensure that each passenger on board occupies a seat or berth and has their safety belt or restraint device properly secured prior to and during taxiing, take-off and landing; and whenever necessary in the interest of safety.

Every person in an aircraft must obey all **lawful commands** which the Pilot-In-Command gives for the purpose of securing the safety of the aircraft and of persons or property carried in the aircraft, or the safety, efficiency or regularity of air navigation.

While in an aircraft, a person must not:

- use any threatening, abusive or insulting words to a member of the crew of the aircraft;
- behave in a threatening, abusive, insulting or disorderly manner to a member of the crew of the aircraft; or
- intentionally interfere with the performance of the crew member's duties.

The Air Navigation Order allows cost sharing between a pilot and passengers subject to the following restrictions:

- The only valuable consideration given or promised for the flight is a contribution to the direct costs of the flight otherwise payable by the pilot in command;
- No more than four persons (including the pilot) are carried;
- No information has been published or advertised before the flight other than (in the case of an aircraft operated by a flying club), advertising within the premises of the flying club, in which case all the persons carried on such a flight who are aged 18 years or over must be members of that flying club;
- No person acting as a pilot is employed as a pilot by, or is in a contract for the provision of services as a pilot with the operator of the aircraft which is being flown.
- 'Direct costs' means the cost directly incurred in relation to a flight, including the cost of fuel, any charges payable for the use of an airfield and any rental or hire fees for the aircraft.
- Additional provisions of the Air Navigation Order allow some remuneration for flights such as air display, charity flights, parachuting, introductory flights and glider towing, subject to specified conditions.

As with other aviation authorities, the UK Civil Aviation Authority takes a very dim view of what is sometimes called 'illegal public transport' and will prosecute pilots who break the rules for non-commercial flights.

## Progress check

45. What UK-specific document contains regulations concerning the operation of non-Part 21 aircraft?
46. What obligation does the ANO place on a Pilot-In-Command in relation to aerodromes?
47. What obligation does the ANO place on a Pilot-In-Command in relation to fuel and oil?
48. Under UK legislation, for what period must a pilot preserve his or her flying logbook?
49. What is the UK minimum time separation for a 'Light' aircraft departing from an intermediate point on a runway behind a 'Medium' wake turbulence category aircraft?
50. Name one land region of the UK which the UK AIP considers to be difficult for Search And Rescue (SAR) operations.
51. What is the UK organisation which investigates aviation accidents and serious incidents?
52. Under UK legislation, are aircraft occupants required to follow the instructions of the Pilot-In-Command?

These questions are intended to test knowledge and reinforce some of the key learning points from this section. In answering these questions, a 'pass rate' of around 80% should be the target.

Model answers are found at page 102.

# OP Progress Check Answers

**OP1 Application of Threat and Error Management**

**OP2 Operation of Aircraft**

**OP 3 Avoidance of Hazards**

**OP4 Search and Rescue Procedures**

**OP5 Accidents and Incidents**

**OP6 Care of Passengers**

**OP7 National Procedures**

# OP Progress Check Answers

## OP1 Application of Threat and Error Management

1. A 'threat' is an external factor outside the control of the pilot which makes the operation of the aircraft more complex or introduces an element of risk. A 'threat' needs to be recognised and managed in order to maintain an acceptable level of safety.
2. Common aviation 'threats' include poor weather, conflict with other aircraft, hostile terrain, aircraft design features and limitations, airfield hazards and equipment malfunction.
3. An 'error' is a pilot action (or lack of action) which leads to a situation the pilot did not intend or expect. An 'error' reduces safety and increases the risk of an incident or accident.
4. Common aviation 'errors' include aircraft handling errors, incorrect operation of the aircraft, procedural errors (eg misreading a checklist, using an incorrect procedure) and communications errors.
5. An undesired aircraft state means that the aircraft is either in the wrong place, at the wrong speed, at the wrong attitude or in the wrong configuration, or in some combination of these undesired states. The most extreme instance of an undesired aircraft state is that of a pilot losing control of the aircraft. Other examples include being too high and too fast on approach, being low on fuel or infringing controlled airspace.
6. Anticipation, recognition and recovery.
7. Situational awareness is a matter of having an accurate understanding of the current situation, the environment around the aircraft and what is likely to occur in the immediate future.
8. According to ICAO, airmanship is "*...the consistent use of good judgment and well-developed skills to accomplish flight objectives.*"

## OP2 Operation of Aircraft

9. Part-NCO
10. A Certificate of Airworthiness (C of A) confirms that an aircraft's design, equipment and maintenance conform to international standards.
11. The Pilot-In-Command (PIC).
12. The Pilot-In-Command (PIC).

13. Before commencing a flight, the Pilot-In-Command must also be familiar with all available meteorological information appropriate to the intended flight. Part-NCO regulations require that the Pilot-In-Command must only commence or continue a VFR flight if the latest available meteorological information indicates that the weather conditions along the route and at the intended destination at the estimated time of use will be at or above the applicable VFR operating minima. In practical terms, this means the VMC minima.

    Before take-off and before landing, the Pilot-In-Command must be satisfied that the weather at the aerodrome or operating site and the condition of the runway will allow a safe take-off or landing as applicable. The latest available weather report should be used for these purposes.

14. The Aircraft Flight Manual (AFM) is a document which contains vital information on the operation of a specific aircraft including information such as limitations, operating procedures, performance data, checklists etc. An individual aircraft will have its own individual AFM, annotated as belonging to a specific aircraft and amended and updated as necessary if the aircraft's equipment changes or operating experience shows that a revision of the AFM is necessary.

15. A Minimum Equipment List (MEL) is a document listing the minimum aircraft equipment required for flight under various conditions, and procedures for dealing with equipment unserviceability.

16. The original Certificate of Registration and the original Certificate of Airworthiness or Permit to Fly.

17. Explosives; ammunition; firearms; large knives or other weapons.

    Camping stoves that run on flammable liquid or gas; diving cylinders pressurised to over 2.8bar or 40psi; fireworks; flammable paint; lighter fuel and lighter refills; 'strike anywhere' matches; oxidisers.

    Corrosive liquids; thinners; poisons; weed killers and insecticides; gas containers; radioactive materials; mercury barometers; batteries.

    Magnetic materials; Portable Electronic Devices (PED).

18. When taking-off and landing at the same aerodrome or landing site, and always remaining in sight of that aerodrome or landing site: the minimum fuel reserve is sufficient fuel and oil to fly the intended route with a reserve of at least 10 minutes at normal cruising altitude.

    In all other circumstances: the minimum fuel reserve is sufficient fuel and oil to fly to the aerodrome of intended landing with a reserve of at least 30 minutes at normal cruising altitude.

19. Part-NCO requires the Pilot-In-Command to check at regular intervals in flight that the amount of usable fuel remaining is not less than the fuel required to proceed to a weather-permissible aerodrome or operating site, plus the planned reserve fuel.

20. The key reference document for fuel and oil grades is the Aircraft Flight Manual (AFM) for the actual aircraft to be flown.

21. No! Operating an aircraft engine using non-approved fuel grades can lead to loss of power, engine and fuel system damage and ultimately engine failure.

22. Refuelling with AVGAS is prohibited under Part-NCO when passengers are on-board, embarking or disembarking an aircraft.
23. Means of measuring and displaying:
    - Magnetic direction;
    - Altitude;
    - Indicated airspeed;
    - Time in hours, minutes and seconds.
24. A first aid kit and a hand-held fire extinguisher.
25. Part-NCO requires that aeroplanes are fitted with an Emergency Locator Transmitter (ELT). If an aircraft was first issued with a Certificate of Airworthiness after 1st July 2008, the ELT must be an 'automatic' type.

    If an aeroplane is certified for a maximum passenger seating of six or less, it is permissible for a passenger or crew member to carry a portable ELT or Portable Locator Beacon (PLB) in place of a fixed ELT.

## OP 3 Avoidance of Hazards

26. In terms of flight safety, a hazard can be considered as a situation, condition or an object which could endanger an aircraft or its occupants, reduce capability, or make the operation of the aircraft significantly more complex.
27. Wake turbulence will occur any time a wing (or rotor blade) is generating lift, it occurs behind the wing of an aircraft (or rotor disc of a helicopter) passing through the air.
28. The ideal atmospheric conditions for wake vortices to persist are zero or very light wind speed in smooth and stable air.
29. In the take-off and departure, approach and landing phases.
30. 5 nautical miles (nm)
31. 2 minutes
32. A helicopter generates stronger wake turbulence than a fixed wing aeroplane of the same weight. Additionally, helicopter wake turbulence is less predictable than that for fixed wing aeroplanes and seems to cover a larger area than that generated by a fixed wing aeroplane of similar size and weight.
33. It is recommended that light aircraft should avoid helicopters hovering or hover-taxiing by a distance equivalent to at least three times the diameter of rotor blades, and stay upwind of the helicopter if possible.

## OP4 Search and Rescue Procedures

34. A Rescue Coordination Centre (RCC) is responsible for organising Search And Rescue (SAR) services and for coordinating search and rescue operations within its area of coverage.

35. Areas that are largely uninhabited, including (for example) moorland, forests and jungles, desert, mountains and high ground, large bodies of water such as river estuaries, the sea and oceans.

36. Part-NCO requires that lifejackets must be carried for all occupants and must be "... *accessible from the seat or berth of the person for whose use it is provided, with a safety belt or a restraint system fastened*". In a single-engine aircraft the normal practice is that lifejackets should worn (but not inflated) by all occupants. Seat cushions are not considered to be flotation devices

37. Require medical assistance.

## OP5 Accidents and Incidents

38. Responsibility for reporting an accident normally rests with the Pilot-In-Command (PIC), or the aircraft operator if the PIC is unable to do so.

39. According to ICAO, the sole objective of the investigation of an accident or incident is the prevention of accidents and incidents. Specifically, it is not the purpose of an accident investigation to allocate blame or liability.

40. An occurrence means any safety-related event which endangers or could endanger an aircraft, its occupants or any other person.

41. Yes.

## OP6 Care of Passengers

42. The Pilot-In-Command (PIC).

43. Yes – Part-NCO requires the Pilot-In-Command to ensure that before (or where appropriate, during) the flight, passengers are given a passenger briefing on emergency equipment and procedures. The guidance material to Part NCO recommends that the passenger briefing should include the locations and use of seat belts and if applicable:

    (1) emergency exits;

    (2) passenger emergency briefing cards;

    (3) lifejackets;

    (4) oxygen dispensing equipment;

    (5) life-rafts; and

    (6) other emergency equipment provided for individual passenger use.

44. The PIC must ensure that, prior to and during taxiing, take-off and landing, and whenever deemed necessary in the interest of safety, "*each passenger on board occupies a seat or berth and has his/her safety belt or restraint device properly secured.*"

## OP7 National Procedures

45. UK regulations for the operation of aircraft are contained in the Air Navigation Order (ANO).
46. The Pilot-In-Command must only use aerodromes and operating sites that are adequate for the type of aircraft and operation.
47. The Pilot-In-Command must ensure sufficient fuel, oil and engine coolant (if required) are carried for the intended flight, and that a safe margin has been allowed for contingencies.
48. A pilot must preserve his or her flying logbook for at least two years from the date of the last entry in it, and produce it to an authorised person within a reasonable time after being requested to do so by that person.
49. 3 minutes.
50. Any of:

    The Scottish Highlands;

    The Hebrides, Orkneys and Shetlands;

    The Pennine Range;

    The Lake District;

    The Yorkshire Moors;

    The Welsh Mountains;

    The Peak District of Derbyshire;

    Exmoor;

    Dartmoor.
51. The Air Accidents Investigation Branch (AAIB).
52. Every person in an aircraft must obey all lawful commands which the Pilot-In-Command gives for the purpose of securing the safety of the aircraft and of persons or property carried in the aircraft, or the safety, efficiency or regularity of air navigation.

# OP Appendix 1 – Abbreviations

Aviation has an unfortunate habit of using hundreds of abbreviations, some more comprehensible than others. Here is a list of abbreviations used in this publication:

| | |
|---|---|
| AAIB | Air Accidents Investigation Branch |
| AFM | Aircraft Flight Manual |
| AIC | Aeronautical Information Circular |
| AIP | Aeronautical Information Publication |
| AMC/GM | Acceptable Means of Compliance and Guidance Material |
| ANO | Air Navigation Order |
| ASI | Airspeed Indicator |
| ATC | Air Traffic Control |
| ATS | Air Traffic Service |
| ATSU | Air Traffic Service Unit |
| AVGAS | **Av**iation **GAS**oline |
| | |
| CAA | Civil Aviation Authority |
| C of A | Certificate of Airworthiness |
| C of R | Certificate of Registration |
| CFIT | Controlled Flight into Terrain |
| CHIRP | Confidential Human Factors Incident Reporting Programme |
| CO | Carbon Monoxide |
| CRD | Child Restraint Device |
| | |
| EASA | European Aviation Safety Agency |
| EFIS | Electronic Flight Instrument System |
| ELT | Emergency Locator Transmitter |
| ETA | Estimated Time of Arrival |
| EU | European Union |
| | |
| FAA | Federal Aviation Authority (of the USA) |
| FCL | Flight Crew Licencing |
| FIR | Flight Information Region |
| FIS | Flight Information Service |
| FL | Flight Level |
| ft | Feet |

| | |
|---|---|
| GA | General Aviation |
| GASCo | General Aviation Safety Council |
| GEN | GENERAL (section of Part-NCO) |
| GHS | Globally Harmonised System |
| | |
| ICAO | International Civil Aviation Organisation |
| IDE | Instruments, Data and Equipment (section of Part NCO) |
| IFR | Instrument Flight Rules |
| IMC | Instrument Meteorological Conditions |
| | |
| kg | Kilogram |
| | |
| m | Metre |
| MEL | Minimum Equipment List |
| MOGAS | **MO**tor **GAS**oline |
| MOR | Mandatory Occurrence Reporting |
| MTOW | Maximum Take-off Mass |
| | |
| NCO | Non-Commercial Operations |
| nm | Nautical MIle |
| | |
| OP | Operational Procedures (section of Part NCO) |
| | |
| PED | Portable Electronic Device |
| PIC | Pilot-In-Command |
| PLB | Personal Locator Beacon |
| POH/FM | Pilots Operating Handbook / Flight Manual |
| POL | Performance and Operating Limitations (section of Part NCO) |
| psi | Pounds per Square Inch |
| | |
| RCC | Rescue Coordination Centre |
| RMZ | Radio Mandatory Zone |
| | |
| SAR | Search and Rescue |
| SOP | Standard Operating Procedures |
| SSR | Secondary Surveillance Radar |
| | |
| TEM | Threat and Error Management |

| | |
|---|---|
| TMG | Touring Motor Glider |
| TMZ | Transponder Mandatory Zone |
| UK | United Kingdom |
| UKAB | UK Airprox Board |
| VFR | Visual Flight Rules |
| VMC | Visual Meteorological Conditions |

# Appendix 2– Supplementary Study Material

This publication is designed to provide the knowledge required to learn Operation Procedures for non-commercial flight operations under Visual Flight Rules (VFR), it is based on the 2015 PPL and LAPL Theoretical Knowledge (TK) Operational Procedures syllabi.

Where a National Aviation Authority (NAA) or training organisation is still working to the 2011 version of the PPL and LAPL Operational Procedures syllabus, there are a small number of topics which are now covered under different TK subjects. If you are preparing for an PPL or LAPL examination under the 2011 syllabus, you are recommended to learn the following supplementary study material, which is presented here in summary form.

## Runway Dimensions

The following definitions can be used to describe runway dimensions and physical characteristics:

- Landing distance available (LDA) – the length of the runway suitable for the ground run of an aeroplane landing.
- Take-off run available (TORA) – the length of runway suitable for the ground run of an aeroplane taking off.
- Accelerate-stop distance available (ASDA) – the length of the take-off run available plus the length of any stopway.
- Take-off distance available (TODA) – the length of the take-off run available plus the length of the clearway available.
- Stopway – an area beyond the runway which can be safely used for stopping an aircraft in the event of an aborted take-off.
- Clearway – an area beyond the runway, free of obstructions and under the control of the airport authorities, over which an aircraft can make part of its initial climb after take-off.

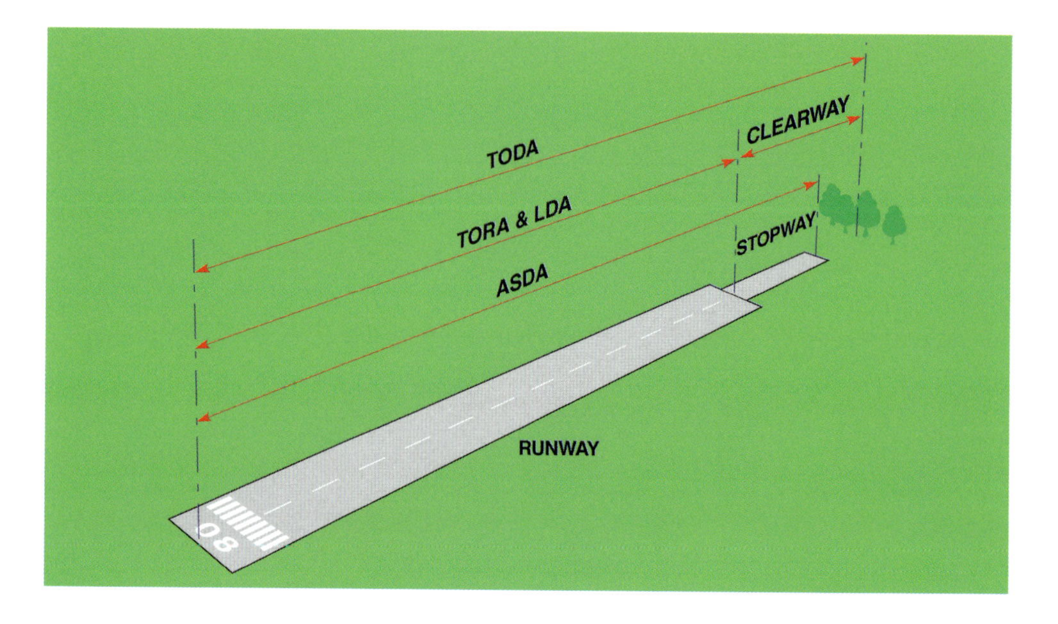

## Runway Holding Points

A runway holding point can be marked with one of more of the following:

- Holding point 'boards' at the side of the taxiway and runway
- A set of solid and broken yellow lines painted across the taxiway
- A line of steady red lights across the taxiway (the 'stop bar')
- Flashing amber 'Runway Guard Lights' next to or across the taxiway

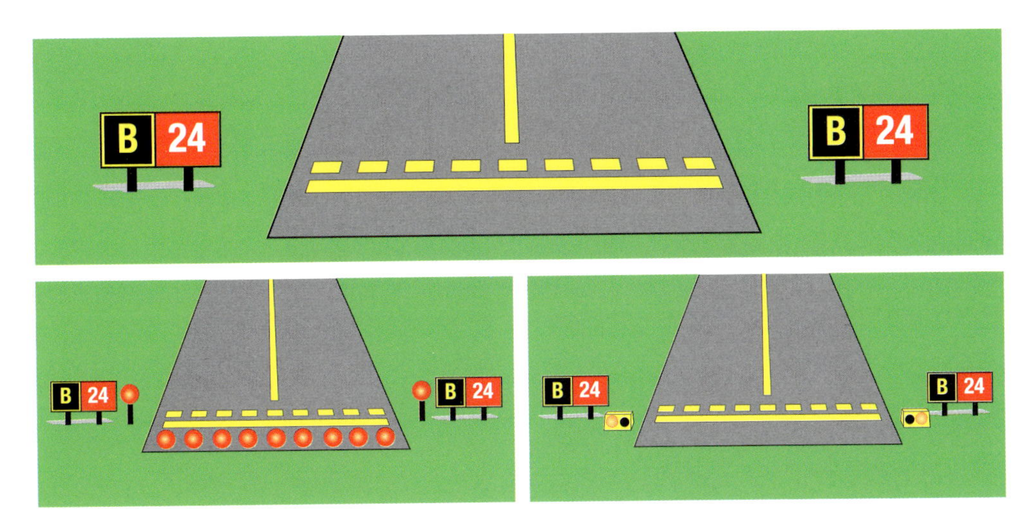


At a controlled aerodrome, the holding point must not be crossed without ATC clearance, and even then only after making a good lookout for aircraft on or approaching the runway. Regardless of ATC clearance, a pilot should not cross an illuminated stop bar.

## Ground to Air Light Signals

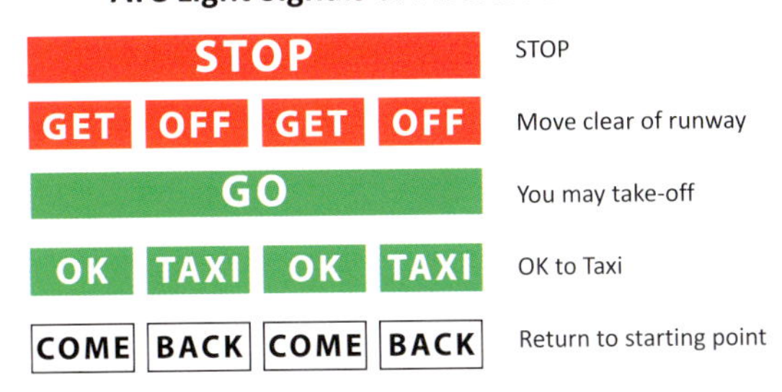


ATC Light Signals to Aircraft in the Air

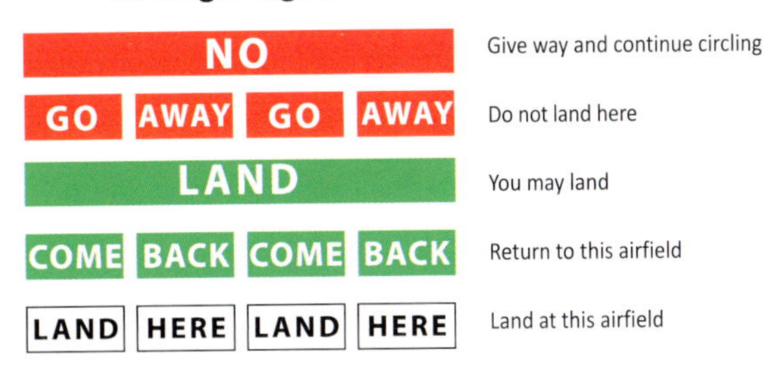

NO
Give way and continue circling
GO AWAY GO AWAY
Do not land here
LAND
You may land
COME BACK COME BACK
Return to this airfield
LAND HERE LAND HERE
Land at this airfield

## Night

'Night' can be defined as the hours between the end of evening civil twilight and the beginning of morning civil twilight. Evening civil twilight ends when the centre of the sun's disc is six degrees below the horizon; morning civil twilight begins when the centre of the sun's disc is six degrees below the horizon.

## Noise Abatement

Noise abatement procedures normally consist of specific routing on arrival and departure (including the circuit) at a specific airfield. These routing (or avoidance areas) are usually notified in the airfield's entry in the Aeronautical Information Publication (AIP) or commercial flight guide.

## Wind shear and Microburst

Wind shear is a sudden change of wind velocity and/or direction over a short distance. Vertical wind shear is a change of horizontal wind direction and/or speed with height, horizontal wind shear is defined as change of horizontal wind direction and/or speed with horizontal distance.

Wind shear, especially at low level, can lead to sudden and significant changes in airspeed and flight path and can represent a serious flight hazard. A sudden change in headwind or tailwind component will cause a rapid, and possibly short-lived, change in airspeed and rate of descent or rate of climb.

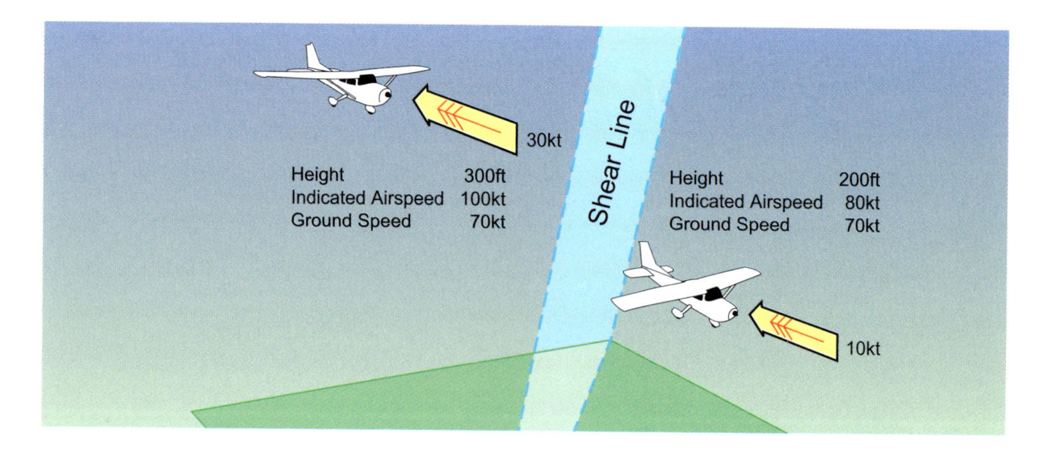


Wind shear is most often associated with thunderstorms, but can also occur around particularly active weather fronts, across a temperature inversion and in turbulence caused by strong winds.

A microburst is a powerful localised area of rain-cooled descending air which, after hitting the ground, spreads out in all directions. Microbursts are most often associated with thunderstorms, but can also occur in association with 'virga' – rain evaporating before reaching the ground. A microburst will often involve strong downdraughts and horizontal winds and can cause severe wind shear.

**A Energy gain**
- increasing headwind
- Airspeed rising
- Rate of descent reduced
- Tendency to go high on glidepath

**B Energy loss**
- reducing headwind and downdraught
- Airspeed falling
- Rate of descent Increased
- Tendency to go low on glidepath

**C Energy loss**
- Increasing tailwind
- Airspeed still falling
- Rate of descent checked by missed approach
- Success depends on power, height and speed reserves available

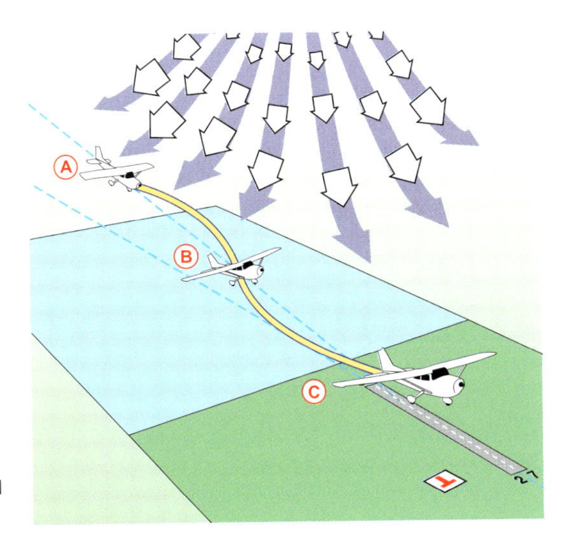


## Emergency and Precautionary Landings

A forced landing is a situation where a pilot is required to make an unavoidable landing (or ditching) and there can be a reasonable expectation of no injuries to those in the aircraft or on the surface.

In the event of an engine failure during cruise in a single-engine aircraft, and subject to the circumstances and emergency checklist, the general sequence of actions may include:

- establish best glide airspeed, assess surface wind, select landing area and plan descent pattern;
- check for causes of failure, in particular: fuel controls, carburettor heat/induction air and ignition switches. If appropriate, attempt re-start;
- make appropriate radio call
- carry-out 'committed checks'

In the event of an engine failure over water and beyond gliding distance of land, it may be appropriate to descend at the best glide endurance airspeed (for maximum time airborne) and to contact ATC (including, if appropriate, using the emergency transponder code 7700) at the beginning of the sequence of actions, in order to increase the chances of being located rapidly.

It is almost always better to plan to ditch parallel to the surface swell of the water, and if possible with an element of headwind.

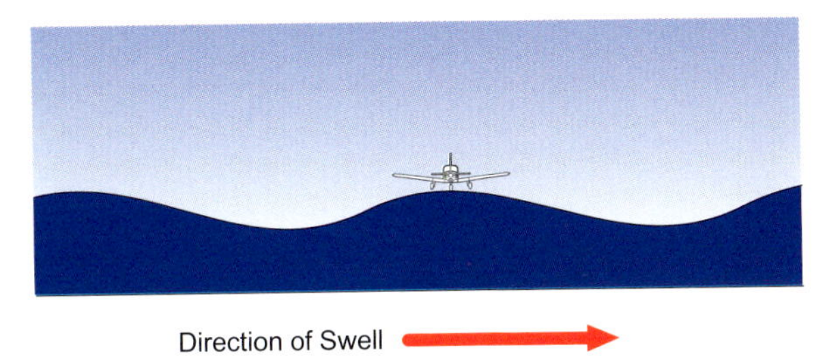


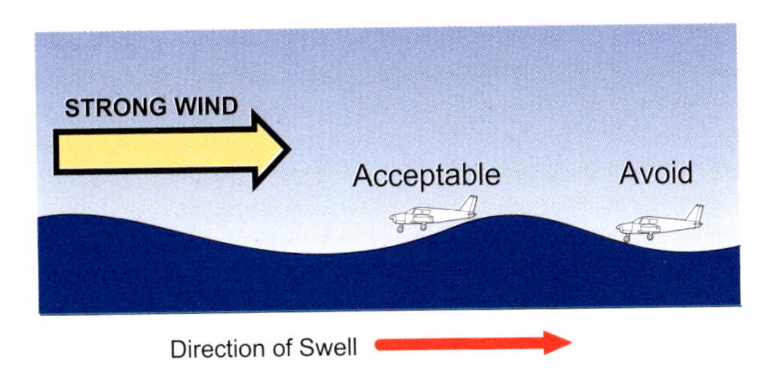

After an emergency landing in a light aircraft, the priority is to evacuate the crew and passengers to a safe position upwind of the aircraft, if possible taking the fire extinguisher and first aid kit on leaving the aircraft. If time permits, all main aircraft systems (fuel, engine, electrical) should be turned off.

## Contaminated Runways

A runway is considered to be contaminated when more than 25% of the runway surface area being used is covered by:

- surface water more than 3mm deep (or by slush, or loose snow, equivalent to more than 3mm of water);
- compacted snow; or
- ice.

A 'wet runway' is one where the runway surface is covered with water, or equivalent, less than 3mm deep, or when there is sufficient moisture on the runway surface to cause it to appear reflective, but without significant areas of standing water.

A 'damp runway' has a surface which is not dry, but the moisture on it does not give it a shiny appearance.

A 'dry runway' is neither wet nor contaminated.

Sometimes, runway condition may be described as 'flooded', meaning that extensive patches of standing water are visible (ie more than 50% of the assessed area is covered by water more than 3mm deep).

The UK CAA advise that the use of a contaminated runway should be avoided if at all possible.

# OP Index

# Notes